The Holy Spirit in Christian Education

SYLVIA LEE, Editor

GOSPEL PUBLISHING HOUSE
SPRINGFIELD, MISSOURI
02–0854

Library of Congress Catalog Card Number 88–80549
International Standard Book Number 0–88243–854–9
Printed in the United States of America

Contents

Foreword

Sometimes you hold an object in your hand and sense greatness. There is a quality that identifies it as a work of craftsmanship, having priceless value.

That is how I felt upon reading *The Holy Spirit in Christian Education*. This book is classic in the true sense of the word. I believe it has the potential of being a watershed, a turning point, a crucial contribution to the future of our Assemblies of God.

One of the miracles of the book is its unity. Individual writers, working only from basic outlines, without the benefit of reading what their fellow authors have written, have produced not an anthology, but a cohesive unit. That reflects the present guidance of the Holy Spirit.

From Ian Hall's concise history of the Pentecostal revival, to General Superintendent G. Raymond Carlson's precise call for a renewed commitment to what the Spirit began in the hearts of our Pentecostal pioneers, there runs one common theme: The Holy Spirit still desires to be active in anointing teachers, illuminating hearts, and opening minds to the Word of God.

It is that dynamic of the convicting, regenerating, infilling, and empowering Spirit that has made the Assemblies of God what we are today. As we come to our 75th year as a movement, we number more than 16 million adherents around the world. It is appropriate that we examine our roots. Our root system strong. Our heritage is vibrant. The same Holy Spirit who guided our early leaders desires to bring renewal and recommitment to the unfinished task.

A careful reading of *The Holy Spirit in Christian Education* will benefit any believer. It will again focus attention on our rich heritage and the great challenge we face in the closing decade of this century.

However, group study and interaction with others involved in a teaching ministry will bring greater benefits. Such a study has the potential to spark fresh revival in your Sunday school and church. We need to recapture the spiritual dynamic that comes from consistent, systematic, small-group study of God's Word. That is Sunday school.

The Pentecostal revival, like the awakenings before it, resulted from a concerted group study of the Bible. The Scriptures illuminated by the same Spirit who inspired holy men to write them are the wellspring of renewal.

We pray for that renewal!

GEORGE A. EDGERLY, SECRETARY
Sunday School Department
Assemblies of God

1

The Pentecostal Revival

IAN R. HALL

The story of the Pentecostal revival is the story of men and women into whose earnest lives God poured His Holy Spirit. It is not the account of an institution tracing its history from inception through changing scenes to modern times, nor is the focus on the development of a doctrine from its earliest perceptions to full-fledged completion. It is the story of people, flawed yet faithful to God as they knew Him; imperfect in understanding and practice yet with a passion for God that would not let go until His promise should be fulfilled in their experience.

At the Beginning

The very name *Pentecostal* takes us back to the beginning of the Christian era, to the Day of Pentecost in Jerusalem where the disciples of the Lord Jesus were awaiting God's gift of the Holy Spirit. "In a few days," Jesus had said prior to His ascension, "you will be baptized with the Holy Spirit" (Acts 1:5). Luke records:

> When the day of Pentecost came, they were all together
> in one place. Suddenly a sound like the blowing of a violent

Ian R. Hall, B.D. and M. Phil., is associate professor in pastoral studies and evangelism at North Central Bible College, Minneapolis, Minnesota.

7

> wind came from heaven and filled the whole house where they were sitting. They saw what seemed to be tongues of fire that separated and came to rest on each of them. All of them were filled with the Holy Spirit and began to speak in other tongues [languages] as the Spirit enabled them (Acts 2:1–4).

Henceforth this first reception of the divine promise was to serve as a model for future experiences of the Holy Spirit baptism. Although the sound of wind and the tongues of fire were seldom if ever repeated, the very fact that the Gentiles at Caesarea spoke "in tongues [other languages]" when they received "the gift of the Holy Spirit" led Peter to realize, "They have received the Holy Spirit just as we have" (Acts 10:45,47). When questions were later raised regarding the propriety of extending this promise to non-Jewish believers the matter was settled by the fact that "the Holy Spirit came on them as he had come on us at the beginning.... God gave them the same gift as he gave us.... God ... showed that he accepted them by giving the Holy Spirit to them, just as he did to us. He made no distinction between us and them" (Acts 11:15,17; 15:8,9).

The consistent reference back to the initial reception on the Day of Pentecost provided the early preachers of the Christian faith with an invariable standard by which to authenticate the experience of believers in future generations and in other lands. "The promise," Peter declared, "is for you and your children and for all who are far off—for all whom the Lord our God will call" (Acts 2:39). On the basis of the Old Testament prophecy of Joel, Peter understood that this outpouring of the Holy Spirit was to continue uninterrupted and unchanged until "the coming of the great and dreadful day of the Lord" (Joel 2:31). The subsequent history of Christianity demonstrates how faithfully that Pentecostal ideal has been realized.

Out Into the World

From its Palestinian home the Christian message quickly penetrated the Roman world and beyond. This extension did, however, bring problems, especially regarding the promised Holy Spirit baptism. Even in apostolic times tension arose over those who wanted to tie the experience of the Spirit to legal observance, making God's promise a reward for superior holiness and evidence of sainthood. Paul stressed that holiness of life is the product not the basis of the indwelling of the Spirit (Galatians 5:16–25; cf. Romans 8:1–13; 1 Corinthians 3:16,17). The promised Holy Spirit is received by faith not good works (Galatians 3:2–5).

Equally problematic were the supernatural manifestations of the Holy Spirit. Some believers were fascinated by spectacular displays while others reacted with great reservation. The Corinthian church, so richly endowed with spiritual gifts—especially vocal manifestations—needed Paul's classic exposition on things of the Spirit to set the situation in order (1 Corinthians 12 to 14). Paul stressed that the cure for abuse is not nonuse but correct use (14:39,40).

The tendency to minimize the value of charismatic manifestations apparently arose very early, within 25 years of the initial outpouring. Thus Paul exhorted the Thessalonian believers, "Do not put out the Spirit's fire; do not treat prophecies with contempt. Test everything. Hold on to the good" (1 Thessalonians 5:19–21). Even a close companion of Paul, the young pastor Timothy, needed repeated encouragement not to neglect his charismatic experience but to fan it into a flame (1 Timothy 4:14; 2 Timothy 1:6).

Despite the clear teachings of Paul, the problem persisted. John needed to explicitly warn one group of believers of the danger of uncontrolled spiritual manifestations (1 John 4:1–6). Yet to other churches he recorded the strongest warnings of the opposite danger of cooling off in spiritual things (Revelation 2:4; 3:15,16).

The polarization of those desiring total freedom for spiritual gifts and those wanting to suppress or even entirely eliminate supernatural manifestations from the church has plagued Christianity since apostolic days. Although the balanced Pentecostal teaching of the apostles was still generally accepted throughout the second century, the extremism of some groups—such as the heretical Gnostics and the fanatical Montanists—ensured the eventual triumph of the ultraconservative group. Ultimately the charismatic experience was virtually excluded from the mainstream of church life.

Most of the early Christian writings have been lost and are known to us only by name or from fragments.[1] However, of those that have survived, most refer to the Holy Spirit baptism and the gifts of the Spirit as a continuing part of the Early Church's experience.[2]

Writing from Rome about A.D. 96, Clement reminded the Corinthian church of that day: "A full outpouring of the Holy Spirit came upon you."[3]

The letters of Ignatius of Antioch, written about A.D. 110 en route to Rome, did much to promote the authority of the bishop and local church leadership, which would eventually lead to the exclusion of the charismatic ministry. Nevertheless, he saw the manifestation of the Spirit as confirming and characterizing the established church official. He reminded the Philadelphian church of a prophetic utterance he had given: "The Spirit made proclamation, saying this: 'Apart from the Bishop do nothing.' "[4]

Throughout the first half of the second century the church was plagued by the problem of false prophets. Both the *Didache (The Teaching of the Lord to the Gentiles through the Twelve Apostles),* believed by many to have been written in Palestine, and *The Shepherd* of Hermas, written in Rome about this time, dealt extensively with the criteria for distinguishing true prophets from the false: "Not everyone speaking in a spirit, is a prophet, only if he has the behavior of the Lord. From their behavior, then, the false prophet and the true prophet are identified."[5]

To Justin Martyr, who died in Rome about A.D. 165, the presence of false prophets confirmed the words of Jesus and did not cancel out the validity of the true gift of the Spirit: "The prophetical gifts remain with us, even to the present time. . . . He said . . . that false prophets and false Christs would appear in his name and deceive many: and so has it come about."[6] Justin also asserted that not only were there in the church in Rome "men and women who possess gifts of the Spirit of God,"[7] but he himself had "been baptized with the Holy Spirit."[8]

Throughout the church of the second century the Pentecostal experience was a vibrant living reality. However, in the latter half of the century in Asia Minor a new movement arose. Although birthed in a genuine Pentecostal outpouring, this movement would later undermine the charismatic ministry of the church. The New Prophecy Movement—later known as Montanism after one of its early leaders, Montanus—was marked by a desire to return to the old standards of holiness in preparation for the soon coming of Christ. Among those caught up in this movement was the recent convert, Montanus of Ardaban in Phrygia, who began to speak in ecstasy, "prophesying in a manner contrary to the constant custom of the Church handed down by tradition from the beginning."[9]

The problem increased as Montanus and his friends refused to submit their charismatic ministry to the evaluation of their peers[10] and justified their actions by rejecting the validity of charismatic prophecy within the institutional church.[11] The result was not just the excommunication of the rebellious Montanists but also the creation of an atmosphere of suspicion toward anyone manifesting spiritual gifts who was not part of the established clergy.

Although bishops like Cyprian of Carthage (248–258), Cyril of Jerusalem (350–386), Basil of Caesarea (370–379), and many of their contemporaries continued to speak of the general diffusion of spiritual gifts among the laity as well as clergy, they believed the Spirit and His gifts were to be transmitted through the clergy to the worthy.[12] The question of who were considered worthy assumed major proportions as the Imperial Church gave way to the Roman Church in the West and the Byzantine Church in the East.

Lights in the Dark Ages

Much of the apostolic faith became overlaid with superstition and tradition as the Dark Ages crept across the old Roman Empire. Ritualism steadily replaced the spontaneity of pre-Imperial Church days, but even ritualism lost its meaning as the institutional church struggled for life against political pressures from rulers and paganism among the people. Nevertheless, the flow of God's Spirit was not staunched. Although the records are incomplete, there is ample evidence that both within the institutional church and outside among the "schismatics" and "heretics"—like the Paulicians and their offspring which survived into the Protestant era—God continued to pour out His Spirit on earnestly seeking believers.

Groups like the Paulicians renounced the traditions of the Medieval Church; e.g., the use of images and relics, the doctrine of transubstantiation, and the practice of infant baptism. They stressed moral purity arising from true repentance and faith in Christ leading to believers' baptism. Subsequently the believers were to receive the *consolamentum,* or Holy Spirit baptism, whereupon they became part of the leadership of the group and were known as *perfecti* (perfected ones), who were able to manifest "extraordinary gifts of the Holy Spirit."[13] They considered themselves to be the true believers preparing the way for the premillennial return of Christ, although the elapse of 12 centuries undoubtedly affected the fervency of their faith at times.

The threat that charismatic groups like the Paulicians posed to the Catholic–Orthodox tradition created an atmosphere of suspicion toward all claiming to be baptized with the Holy Spirit. About A.D. 1000 the official Roman Catholic service book, the *Rituale Romanum,* in the section "Exorcism of the Possessed," gave several indices for distinguishing demon possession from mental illness:

> Signs of possession are the following: ability to speak
> with some facility in a strange tongue or to understand it

when spoken by another; the faculty of divulging future or hidden events; display of powers which are beyond the subject's age and natural condition; and various other indications which, when taken together as a whole, pile up the evidence.[14]

With this attitude toward the *charismata* prevailing in the institutional church, it is hardly surprising that each successive wave of spiritual blessing, while initially producing examples of charismatic manifestations, resulted in the movement of the revived laity outside the church and into the rival sects. Only among monastics like Bernard of Clairvaux (1090–1153), Hildegard of Bingen (1098–1179), Joachim of Fiore (1135–1202), Dominic Guzman (1170–1221), Francis of Assisi (1182–1226), and Antony of Padua (1195–1231), and missionaries, such as Vincent Ferrer (1350–1419) and Francis Xavier (1506–1552), were *charismata* to flourish as marks of sainthood or, at least, superior holiness.

The Return to Apostolic Faith

Although the preceding millennium (A.D. 500–1500) had seen successive waves of spiritual revival affecting larger or smaller groups both within and outside the Catholic–Orthodox Church, it was not until the great 16th-century Reformation that these outpourings of God's Spirit not only renewed the spiritual life of the revived but also sparked a restoration of scriptural truth. Steadily the revived church moved closer to apostolic faith and experience.

With the Reformation came the restoration of the biblical truth of justification by faith; in the Puritan Awakening came the concept of the church as a gathered community of believers; in the Great (Wesleyan) Awakening, the second blessing; in the Second Great Awakening, the missionary vision of the Great Commission; in the 1825–1842 wave, the second coming of Christ; in the midcentury revival, the concept of Christian holiness through the fullness of the Holy Spirit; leading to the restoration of Pentecostal power in the decade of revival at the beginning of the 20th century.

These four centuries of revival were also marked by many instances of charismatic manifestations, as though God were steadily and patiently giving the earnestly seeking believer a foretaste of the blessings to come with the fuller restoration of apostolic Christianity.

John Wesley inherited much of his religious experience from the Moravians, among whom the *charismata* had sporadically occurred.[15] He also expressed a highly favorable opinion of the Montanists[16] and believed that the *charismata* had been lost to the church generally because of a "cooling" of love.[17] However, there was no widespread outbreak of spiritual gifts during the Great Awakening and even a skepticism of the few instances known. Of all Wesley's colleagues, only John Fletcher of Madeley (1729–1785), and his biographer Joseph Benson, seemed ready both to express the Wesleyan teaching on the second blessing in terms of "receiving the Holy Ghost"[18] and to insist that the *charismata* might be available in their day.[19] It was not until the middle of the 19th century that Pentecostal terminology was generally adopted by the Wesleyan holiness movement, which prepared the way for the modern Pentecostal outpouring.

The early 19th-century revivals were marked by several outbreaks of the Pentecostal experience, particularly among those expecting a full restoration of apostolic faith and vitality at that time. Similar outbreaks continued throughout the 19th century as waves of revival swept across the evangelical world, especially in North America and Europe. Although charismatic groups were born from these outbreaks (e.g., the Gift Adventists of New England, the Christian Union in Tennessee, and the Holiness Baptists in the Carolinas and Georgia), the main impetus for the full restoration of the apostolic faith was to come from the midcentury holiness revival.

Preparation for Another Pentecost

The publication of the British Methodist William Arthur's

book *The Tongue of Fire* in 1856 both sparked the revival of 1857 and helped set its Pentecostal tone.[20] Up to this point Wesleyans and Oberlin Perfectionists, following Charles Finney, had customarily spoken of the second blessing in terms of sanctification and perfection, but Arthur took the Book of Acts, and particularly the Day of Pentecost, as a model for his exposition, effectively stimulating a general quest for a new Pentecost.

By 1870 the second blessing was commonly being referred to as "the Baptism of the Holy Ghost,"[21] and the adjective *Pentecostal* expressed the mind-set of holiness believers. The result was that the traditional Wesleyan concept of purity was augmented by a new element—power. For the majority, purity and power represented the negative and positive aspects of the one experience.

Others were of a Reformed, rather than a Wesleyan, persuasion (e.g., D.L. Moody and his successor R.A. Torrey). They diminished the role of cleansing and stressed the baptism with the Spirit as providing power for service and victorious Christian living—the "overcoming life."

A third approach was to separate the experiences into regeneration, then sanctification, followed by a third, the baptism with the Spirit for power (sometimes called the baptism of fire). Hence groups advocating this approach often adopted the title Fire-Baptized Holiness Church.

Although the *charismata* were not directly linked to the developing Pentecostal terminology at this point, there was a rising interest in divine healing. This particularly resulted from the work of Charles Cullis, an Episcopalian physician in Boston, who established a faith healing home in 1862 and, 14 years later, opened the Faith Training College. Staffed by outstanding holiness teachers, such as W.E. Boardman, A.B. Earle, Daniel Steele, and W. McDonald, the college was devoted to presenting Christ as Savior from all sin and sickness.

The concept of healing in the Atonement, or divine healing as its advocates preferred to call it, became the dominant theology both in the holiness movement at the turn of the century and in the infant Pentecostal movement. The clear teaching of balanced advocates like A.B. Simpson and A.J. Gordon avoided the dangers of extremism by recognizing that all the benefits of the Atonement are not received in this life; the believer receives only the firstfruits of the full harvest to come.

The Apostolic Faith Restored

In 1894 the bishops of the Methodist Episcopal Church South proposed a moratorium on the proclamation of the second blessing within Methodism until the leading holiness teachers could agree as to the scriptural evidence whereby a person could know he had received this blessing. On the one hand, each preacher seemed to expect different indices from the recipients—prostration or leaping, laughing or weeping, ecstatic thrills or even visions—and anathematized his rivals. On the other hand, many of the recipients who had the most spectacular manifestations subsequently discovered that their experiences of entire sanctification were short-lived.

As sensible as the Methodist bishops' request was, many holiness preachers interpreted it as abandoning the true Wesleyan position and left to form independent missions, new denominations, or simply to become itinerant evangelists. Among these was a young Iowan, Charles Fox Parham (1873–1929), formerly pastor of the Methodist Episcopal Churches in Eudora and Linwood, Kansas.

In the fall of 1898 Parham felt impressed to establish the Bethel Divine Healing Home on the corner of Fourth and Jackson Streets in Topeka, Kansas. In addition to alleviating the suffering of the sick and needy who came to reside in the home, he also pastored an independent holiness mission and published a biweekly paper *The Apostolic Faith*.

In 1900, Parham became convinced that he should open a Bible college that fall to "operate on Faith lines" and to "fit men and women to go to the ends of the earth to preach 'this Gospel of the Kingdom.' "[22] About 40 ministers and Bible stu-

dents gathered in the old mansion, "Stone's Folly," to open
Bethel Bible College in October 1900. By December they had
examined the subjects of repentance, conversion, consecration,
sanctification, healing, and the soon coming of Christ. In Parham's own words:

> Having heard so many different religious bodies claim
> different proofs as the evidence of their having the Pen-
> tecostal baptism, I set the students at work studying out
> diligently what was the Bible evidence of the baptism of
> the Holy Ghost, that we might go before the world with
> something that was indisputable because it tallied abso-
> lutely with the Word.[23]

On his return from 3 days of meetings in Kansas City on
December 31, Parham summoned the students to the chapel
for their report. To his astonishment they all agreed that "when
the Pentecostal blessing fell, the undisputable proof on each
occasion was, that they spoke with other tongues."[24] The next
day, following a singularly blessed watchnight service, as the
students were seeking this fuller baptism in the Holy Spirit,
Agnes Ozman became the first to receive the Holy Spirit with
the expected evidence of glossolalia:

> It was nearly seven o'clock on this first of January that
> it came into my heart to ask Brother Parham to lay his
> hands upon me that I might receive the gift of the Holy
> Spirit. It was as his hands were laid upon my head that
> the Holy Spirit fell upon me and I began to speak in tongues,
> glorifying God.[25]

The entire student body spent the next 3 days seeking the
same experience. Miss Ozman encouraged them to seek the
Holy Spirit not tongues, since she was not yet sure that all
would receive this evidence. Returning from preaching in the
local Free Methodist Church on January 3, Parham went to
the prayer room:

> The door was slightly ajar, the room was lit with only
> coal oil lamps. As I pushed open the door I found the room

was filled with a sheen of white light above the brightness of the lamps. Twelve ministers, who were in the school of different denominations, were filled with the Holy Spirit and spoke with other tongues.[26]

Overcome by this "evidence of the restoration of Pentecostal power," Parham was also baptized with the Holy Spirit that very night and within a few days almost the whole student body had also received this Baptism. The first attempts at spreading the news were generally greeted by curiosity and then opposition on the part of the secular media and the religious world. By early 1903 only Rev. and Mrs. Parham and his wife's sister Lilian Thistlethwaite were left of the original "apostolic faith" group, as they called themselves.

A series of successful meetings in the spring of 1903 in Nevada, Missouri, and then in El Dorado Springs, Missouri, prepared the way for the immensely successful ministry in Galena, Kansas, from October 1903 to January 15, 1904. Over 800 were converted, more than 1000 healed of various diseases, and many hundreds baptized in the Holy Spirit with the evidence of speaking in other languages.[27] From Galena, the message spread throughout the neighboring communities in Kansas, Missouri, and Oklahoma, but the most significant development was the invitation to carry the apostolic faith message to Orchard, Texas.

Commencing his meetings on Easter Sunday, 1905, Parham found Texas ripe for revival, as indeed was much of the Western world.[28] The news quickly spread to nearby Houston, where the Holiness Church in the suburb of Brunner, led by Pastor W.F. Carothers, became the main center for the crusade the following July. As the meetings in Galena, Kansas, had been precipitated by the miraculous healing of Mary Arthur, so the Houston Crusade in the Bryan Hall was marked by the healing of Mrs. Delaney, a lawyer's wife who had been paralyzed in a streetcar accident.

By the winter of 1905, some 25,000 apostolic faith believers were reported in Texas alone[29] and another Bible school was opened in Houston to train ministers for the growing number of apostolic faith missions opening throughout the state. To this time almost all the people involved had been white, but it was a black holiness preacher, William J. Seymour, a student at the Houston Bible school, whose ministry would precipitate the worldwide spread of the apostolic faith message.

Azusa Street and Beyond

Neeley Terry, a member of a black Nazarene mission on Santa Fe Street in Los Angeles, California, was visiting Houston when she met William Seymour. Miss Terry was so impressed with him that on her return she pressed the interim pastor, Mrs. Julia Hutchinson, to invite Seymour to hold meetings with a view to his becoming the pastor. According to the earliest accounts of Seymour's ministry, he traveled to Los Angeles in early February 1906 and ministered in the Nazarene mission with some acceptability before his insistence on tongues as the evidence of the baptism in the Holy Spirit led to the church being locked against him.[30]

Rejected by the holiness believers, Seymour continued regular prayer meetings in the home of Richard and Ruth Asberry, Baptist relatives of Neeley Terry. Early in April, Lucy Farrow and J.A. Warren from Houston joined him, and on the evening of April 9, 1906, Pentecost came to the small group of praying believers. Seymour himself did not receive the Holy Spirit baptism until April 12.

To accommodate the growing crowds, Seymour moved the services to a former Methodist church at 312 Azusa Street that had more recently served as a livery stable and tenement house. It would be the center of revival for the next 3 years. From Azusa Street the apostolic faith message spread along the West Coast to Canada, the Midwest, the Southeast, the Northeast, then to Europe, Latin America, and Southern Africa, as earnest seekers after revival heard of what God was doing and either visited the mission in person or simply "prayed through" on the basis of the news that Pentecost had truly come again.

Initially, as in the Texas work of Parham, the apostolic faith message had three parts: salvation, sanctification, and the Holy Spirit baptism. However, as believers came into the Pentecostal experience from a Reformed background—which taught that sanctification was progressive—disquiet was felt over the teaching of sanctification as a crisis experience following conversion.

In 1910 controversy erupted that was to divide the apostolic faith movement into two camps: those following the traditional holiness teaching with the addition of the Holy Spirit baptism, represented by the original apostolic faith groups and the holiness-Pentecostal bodies in the southeast; and those primarily independent missions accepting the "finished work" concept.

The Birth of the Assemblies of God

By 1914 the "finished work" missions had begun to realize that without some kind of organizational link with like-minded believers, they were vulnerable to division and deception. The holiness Pentecostals had existing denominations which gave them structure and cohesion, but the independent missions were prey to powerful personalities or even outright tricksters. Being part of a legally incorporated body also offered other advantages, such as reduced rail fares for clergy and freedom from military conscription for young ministers.

In December 1913, groups of ministers in the Midwest formerly associated with Parham's apostolic faith group and with the predominantly black Church of God in Christ, issued a call in the *Word and Witness* paper published by M.M. Pinson for a "General Convention of Pentecostal Saints and Churches of God in Christ" to meet together in Hot Springs, Arkansas, to consider five subjects.

> First—We come together that we may get a better understanding of what God would have us teach, that we may do away with so many divisions. . . .
> Second—. . . that we may know how to conserve the work . . . in home and foreign lands.
> Third—. . . that we may get a better understanding of the needs of each foreign field . . . .

Fourth—Many of the saints have felt the need of chartering the Churches of God in Christ. . . .

Fifth—We may have a proposition to lay before the body for a general Bible Training School with a literary department for our people.[31]

Many feared the organization would stifle the work of the Holy Spirit, but from the opening of the convention on Thursday, April 2, 1914 it became increasingly obvious that God was in it. While not all of the over 300 attending the opening meetings became part of The General Council of the Assemblies of God, even many of those who rejected the call for a cooperative body later formed a separate organization of their own. From the outset it was determined that the General Council should be a voluntary cooperative fellowship of sovereign assemblies offering mutual recognition of ministers and ministries deemed worthy of the support of the "Pentecostal, Apostolic Faith and Church of God in Christ group."

Although the Bible was stated to be "the all-sufficient rule for faith and practice," it quickly became apparent that in view of the impinging doctrinal issues (such as the Jesus Only teaching) a fuller statement of faith would be needed. The Statement of Fundamental Truths was adopted at the Fourth General Council in St. Louis, Missouri, in October 1916.

"From this humble, small beginning the work was destined to grow, until the combined influence of workers together would spread around the world. The Assemblies of God was on the way!"[32]

NOTES

[1]Edgar J. Goodspeed, *A History of Early Christian Literature,* ed. Robert M. Grant (Chicago: University of Chicago Press, 1966).

[2]R.A. Kydd, *Charismatic Gifts in the Early Church* (Peabody: Hendrickson, 1984).

[3]*1 Clement* 2:2.

[4]Ignatius *Philadelphians* 7:1, 2.

[5]*Didache* 11:8 cf. Hermes *Shepherd,* Mandate 11.

[6]Justin *Dialogue With Trypho.*

[7]Ibid.

[8]Ibid.

[9]Eusebius *Ecclesiastical History,* V. 16.

[10]Ibid.

[11]Irenaeus *Against Heresies,* III xi. 9.

[12]Cyprian *Epistles,* LXXIII. 5; Cyril *Catechetical Lectures,* XVII. 35–37; Basil *Shorter Rules,* CCIV.

[13]Edward Gibbon, *History of Christianity* (New York: Peter Eckler, 1923; reprint ed., Salem, N.H.: Ayer Co., Publishers, 1972).

[14]P.T. Weller, ed. and trans., *The Roman Ritual* (Milwaukee, Wisc.: Bruce, 1952) Vol. II.

[15]G. Williams and Edith Waldvogel, "A History of Speaking in Tongues," *The Charismatic Movement* (Grand Rapids: Eerdmans, 1975).

[16]Ibid., p. 80.

[17]T. Jackson, ed., *The Works of John Wesley* (London: Epworth, 1829–1831, 3rd ed.), VII. 27.

[18]D. Dayton, "The Doctrine of the Baptism of the Holy Spirit," *Wesley Theological Journal* 13 (September 1978).

[19]Williams and Waldvogel, "A History of Speaking in Tongues."

[20]Dayton, "The Doctrine of the Baptism of the Holy Spirit."

[21]The title of Asa Mahan's definitive work on sanctification.

[22]Sarah E. Parham, *The Life of Charles F. Parham* (Joplin, Mo.: Tri–State Printing Company, 1930).

[23]Ibid.

[24]Ibid.

[25]Ibid.

[26]Ibid.

[27]Reported in the *Cincinnati Inquirer,* January 27, 1904.

[28]See J.E. Orr, *The Flaming Tongue* (Chicago: Moody Press, 1973) for fuller details.

[29]William W. Menzies, *Anointed To Serve* (Springfield, Mo.: Gospel Publishing House, 1971), p. 48.

[30]William J. Seymour, *The Apostolic Faith,* 1 and 4 (September and December 1906); B.F. Lawrence, *The Apostolic Faith Restored* (St. Louis, Mo: Gospel Publishing House, 1916); D.J. Nelson, "For Such a Time as This: The Story of W.J. Seymour and the Azusa Street Renewal" (Ph.D. dissertation, University of Birmingham, U.K., 1981).

[31]Menzies, *Anointed To Serve,* pp. 93,94.

[32]Ibid., p. 105.

2

Our Sunday Schools—
Spirit Powered

BYRON KLAUS

The history of the church in America in the 19th and 20th centuries is both complex and exciting. However, any honest church historian would be hard-pressed to tell the story of church growth in America, without seeing the Sunday school as integral to that growth. The fact the Sunday school has been crucial to church growth in America is affirmed by both theological liberals and conservatives.[1]

The Beginnings of Sunday School

The story of the modern Sunday school begins in 1780, with Robert Raikes in Gloucester, England. The Industrial Revolution had brought radical change to England, and Raikes observed that the greatest suffering occurred among the children trapped in factories and slums. Raikes' Sunday schools were not a tool of the local church. Their goal was to reach the very dregs of society—those a callous England had forgotten—with hope. He wished to teach them "reading, writing, morals, and manners" based on God's Word. For his efforts he was called "Bobby Wild Goose and his Ragged Regiment," but he persevered. When he died in 1811 over 400,000 children were enrolled in Sunday school.

Byron Klaus, D. Min., is director of graduate studies at Southern California College, Costa Mesa, California.

Wesley Willis suggests that Sunday school's impact on England in the 18th century brought very noticeable results. The Sunday school movement, along with the Wesley and Whitefield revivals, spared England from the terror of the French Revolution. It was a stimulus to awakening the upper classes in England to their responsibility to the poor. It paralleled the first great era of missionary sending from England and produced the religious literature needed for world evangelization.[2]

The Sunday school found a warm reception in America. The frontier revivalism that is so much a part of American church history has Sunday school interwoven in it. From circuit-riding preachers like Francis Asbury to American Sunday School Union evangelists like Stephen Paxson, Sunday school provided a key link to religious life and the growth of the church in America.[3]

About the time of the founding of the Assemblies of God in 1914, the international Sunday school movement reached its peak. Theological liberalism and a shift from a lay-centered movement to professional religious educators took its toll in years to come.[4] However, the Sunday school as a serious contributor to church growth has continued to play a key role among conservative groups. Even though evangelicals will affirm that the Sunday school has played such a crucial role in church growth, the modern Sunday school movement seems to be in serious need of renewal.

The Sunday school has been hurt almost as much by those who love it as by those who hate it. Some abandon Sunday school (without a functional replacement) while others champion it as the lifeblood of the church. Some people would label the Sunday school as the "most wasted hour of the week." Others suggest that Sunday school is the singular reason they are Christians today.

This being the case, in this chapter we will try to understand the history of the Sunday school so we can evaluate the present and plan for the future.

The Assemblies of God and Sunday School

From its inception, the Assemblies of God has been a supporter of the Sunday school. Although the Fellowship did not develop its own Sunday School Department until 1935, the Sunday school was seen as essential to personal Christian growth and evangelistic outreach.[5]

As early as 1914, Mrs. J.R. Flower was preparing lesson comments on the International Sunday School lessons for publication in the *Evangel*. J.W. Welch (second general superintendent of the Assemblies of God) wrote in 1915, "No pastor can neglect this opportunity of promoting Sunday schools or be indifferent to the needs of children and young people within the realm of his influence."[6] By 1919 steps were being taken to print literature.

Ralph Riggs (who later became general superintendent) wrote in 1931, "Next to the church services and the care of the adults of the congregation, without doubt the most important of all phases of church life is the Sunday School."[7] Riggs also wrote a Sunday school organization manual in 1933.

Myer Pearlman provides a glimpse into the value early Assemblies of God leadership placed on Sunday school. In 1935 he wrote, "He who has responded to the call to teach a Sunday School class has indeed chosen a great work, for his call carries with it the privilege and responsibility of co-operating with God in the molding of Christian character and the imparting of spiritual knowledge. In a very real sense he has been called to the ministry."[8]

Significant years of Assemblies of God church growth took place after World War II. These were also boom years for the Sunday school. Attendance at the 11th annual National Sunday School Convention in St. Louis in 1954 was over 11,000. Although Sunday school attendance has leveled off in recent years, growing Assemblies of God churches are committed to Sunday school. The International Christian Education Association annually awards the fastest-growing Sunday schools in each of the 50 states. Assemblies of God schools continue to be a significant portion of those honored.

To be truly committed to a ministry, particularly over a protracted period of time, we must continually examine its original purpose. Times change but biblical norms do not. Properly supporting biblical norms (including disciple-making) with relevant forms of ministry requires regular evaluation. The analysis of present needs should include an understanding of the motivation behind a ministry's conception. What is the genius of Sunday school and why has it endured as such a force over 200 years and during the entirety of Assemblies of God history?

Objectives for the Sunday School

Sunday school in the Assemblies of God has endured and made valuable contributions for a number of reasons. Let's look at those contributions in light of the objectives established by the national Sunday School Department.

1. *Salvation*—To help each student receive Christ
2. *Biblical knowledge*—To help each student hear, understand, believe, and obey the Bible
3. *Spirit-filled life*—To help each student receive the baptism in the Holy Spirit and maintain a daily walk with the Spirit
4. *Christian growth*—To help each student grow into Christian maturity
5. *Personal commitment*—To help each student totally commit his life to the will of God
6. *Christian service*—To help each student find and fulfill his place of service as a member of the body of Christ, the Church
7. *Christian living*—To help each student apply Christian principles to every relationship of life[9]

The first objective, *salvation,* is implied in the evangelistic thrust Sunday school has historically taken. From the frontier Sunday schools started by Stephen Paxson, to the Sunday school started by D.L. Moody in the Chicago slums, evangelism through education has been at the core of Sunday school ministry. Assemblies of God Sunday schools have historically seen the need for making evangelism central to all they do. The beginnings of many Assemblies of God churches were combination Sunday school/preaching points that eventually became congregations.

Countless Assemblies of God members have responded to a salvation invitation given in the Sunday school. Pastor Richard Dresselhaus says, "Evangelism is the key to building the work of God, and the Sunday school becomes the arm that turns the key."[10] Radiant Life Curriculum has focused this evangelistic thrust in its lesson plans by providing both methodology and training for concluding each week's lesson with an evangelistic invitation.

The pioneer spirit of Robert Raikes and D.L. Moody—to reach the children caught in urban blight—is being kept alive by people like Bill Wilson, pastor of Metro Assembly in Brooklyn, New York. This church ministers to thousands of children every week in New York slums. Despite bodily injury, continual harrassment and danger, and the murder of a staff member, this church continues to bring hope to a forgotten people.

Countless other stories could be told of Assemblies of God Sunday schools—both rural and urban—that burn with a passion for souls. Some are "prettier" than others, but all are seeking to do what the Sunday school has done for nearly 200 years: provide an *entry point* into Christian faith and *personal support* in Christian growth. Since the vast majority of our membership still enter the church through the Sunday school, this ministry should be taken seriously in any church seeking to grow.[11]

The nurturing of *Christian growth and personal commitment* are also important Sunday school objectives. Dr. Billie Davis suggests four reasons why the Sunday school class is an ideal setting in which to achieve these goals.[12]

First, the Sunday school class can provide a context for comparison. As members share experiences and their interpretations, the group can help them gain new insights.

Second, the Sunday school class can develop cohesiveness

(*koinonia,* community). Warm, accepting relationships lift self-esteem and encourage members to risk revealing needs and requesting prayer.

Third, the Sunday school class can impose social standards by reinforcing positive behavior and discouraging unwholesome attitudes.

Fourth, the Sunday school class can define reality for its members from a scriptural point of view.

As scriptural teaching and Christian testimony are welded together in an atmosphere of trust and openness to the Holy Spirit, the Sunday school class can effectively minister to the needs of its members.

David Torgerson, former secretary of the Sunday School Department, notes that the Assemblies of God's rapid growth has brought into sharp focus the matter of effectively relating to the new Christian and the visitor. People coming into our Fellowship today have considerably less Christian background than did newcomers 25 to 30 years ago. In addition to making the newcomer feel welcome, the Sunday school class can provide a loving community in which the Christian growth and commitment of each individual can occur.[13]

The apostle Paul's use of the metaphor "body of Christ" is no small clue to the formational power of a Sunday school class. Ephesians 4:11–16 describes the potential of a contemporary Sunday school. Surveys of growing Sunday schools in our Fellowship reveal that the Sunday school is a unique structure that builds cohesiveness among members. This provides the church with the sensitivity to respond to its members' spiritual needs before they become overwhelming.

Christian service is another objective of Assemblies of God Sunday schools. No other ministry of the church involves more laypeople in productive service than the Sunday school. The Sunday school began as a lay movement and its great heroes have been laypeople. As stated earlier, its decline internationally can be directly linked to its dominance by professional religious educators.

Christian service, as an expression of our response to the claims of Christ on our life, is crucial to our Christian growth. Part of the genius of Sunday school is it gives ample opportunity to scores of people to be involved in service.

In 1935, Marcus Grable, a layman with a burden for Sunday school, was appointed the first promotions director of the national Sunday School Department. Grable's vision was of a mighty lay movement to win and nurture children. As the adult education movement emerged in the United States, he also championed the idea of adult Sunday school classes, attempting to lay to rest the idea that Sunday school was only for children.[14]

Because the Sunday school reaches the widest spectrum of people in any local church, it provides a gold mine of ministry possibilities for people gifted and burdened in scores of areas. And their examples of service provide models for others to follow. Missions education in the Sunday school through Boys and Girls Missionary Crusade (BGMC) plants seeds for future generations of cross-cultural workers.

Assemblies of God Sunday schools also include in their objectives, *biblical knowledge and the Spirit-filled life.* Our society is awash in a sea of nonbiblical values. There has never been a time when people needed more to be nurtured in their knowledge of the Bible and hunger for God. James' epistle suggests that obedience to Christ is the only proper response to our biblical knowledge (James 1:22–25).

Knowing what we believe and being able to defend our faith have always been requirements for the Christian. The demands of the remaining decade of the 20th century should grip us deeply as we look at the scores of new converts who are being born into the Kingdom and desperately need nurturing. The *content* of the authoritative Word of God taught in the *context* of a small caring community of believers, such as a Sunday school class, is a powerful tool.

In Assemblies of God Sunday schools, hunger and thirst for God's Word can be nurtured by a deep commitment to the Spirit-filled life. The baptism in the Holy Spirit, held so dear by our Fellowship, is a key to the believer's spiritual maturity. All Bible study should teach the scriptural reasons for what we believe. The Spirit-filled life, with its doorway of the baptism in the Holy Spirit, makes for powerful Christian living.

Truths about the baptism in the Holy Spirit can be taught and discussed in the Sunday school class. This setting—where people know and are known—may provide the most open atmosphere for people to receive the baptism in the Spirit. Assemblies of God Sunday schools with their dual emphasis on Bible knowledge and the Spirit-filled life provide believers with power to obey the Word of God.

Countless Sunday school teachers are the unsung heroes of our Fellowship. They have faithfully taught the Word of God and instructed believers, young and old, on the baptism in the Holy Spirit. Without fanfare, they have prayed for people to receive this mighty Baptism. Only eternity will tell the numbers of people who have received such care and concern by these servants of God. Triumphant living in our pluralistic society, as well as global evangelization, depend on such Sunday school classes being restored to their proper place.

The task our Lord left us included teaching new disciples to obey everything He had commanded (Matthew 28:19,20). The complementary objectives of *Bible knowledge and the Spirit-filled life* are the bedrock of the Pentecostal faith. We do not learn the Word of God merely to accumulate information and argue over theological concepts. But, through the authoritative Word, we learn to know a God who desires to empower a people for His gracious purpose. Assemblies of God Sunday schools must continue to renew their commitment to know Him and make Him known.

The seventh objective of the Assemblies of God Sunday school is *Christian living.* The Assemblies of God has a deep heritage as a holiness people. Christian living is holy living. Our society, on the other hand, has moved beyond immorality to amorality. There is no longer any acknowledgment of a basis for morality. Hegelian philosophy has injected poison into western civilization for such a protracted period of time that hopeless nihilism is rampant.

Historically, the Sunday school has been a foundational teaching point for morality. Robert Raikes tried to penetrate the immorality of the Industrial Revolution with morality based on God's Word. Sunday school enthusiasts of the mid-19th century, like Henry Ward Beecher, spoke fervently for the Sunday school as a "reservoir of moral influence" carried into neighborhoods, streets, and households.[15]

Although the holiness tradition can at times lead to legalism, we should not despise biblical emphasis on holy living. Children and adults who enter a Sunday school classroom are deeply impacted by the world they live in. A supportive community of believers where God's Word and its standard for morality can be taught and discussed is vital.

Early Assemblies of God leaders realized the Sunday school was a place where holy living could be modeled by holy men and women of God. In 1931, Ralph Riggs wrote, "The higher purpose of Sunday school work is for ... teachers to exert a strong personal influence over the pupils, to mold their characters and lead them to Christ."[16] The power of a teacher's life to model Christian living is significant.

Noted Christian educator Howard Hendricks tells of a Sunday school teacher he met while speaking at a convention in Chicago's Moody Memorial Church. The teacher was 83 years old and had a class of 13 junior high boys in a church with only 65 members. She had traveled all night on a bus to come to the convention.

Hendricks asked why she had come such a long distance. Her response was, "To learn something that would make me a better teacher."

She had a passion to communicate her encounter with Jesus Christ. As she modeled Christian living, her life spoke volumes to countless young boys. In her tenure as a Sunday school teacher, 84 of those junior high boys entered full-time vocational ministry.[17]

As Sunday school teachers, we dare not cast aside the opportunity to model for hungry people the powerful life we have in Christ.

A Movement at the Crossroads

Those who study religious movements say the Assemblies of God is at a crossroads. If we are compared with other revivalist movements it would seem we have reached the apex; decline is on our horizon. Other groups like us have come and gone. What will help us endure? How can the Assemblies of God rewrite theories on revival movements?

These questions require prayerful reflection and study. Our heritage is in our favor. We are people from the other side of the tracks, the "disinherited."[18] Our modest beginnings are in part why God has blessed us. Now we have respectability in the Christian world, but will that hinder or help us in our desire to see God continue to pour out His blessings on us? Our openness to the Spirit is our only hope that we can and will see a spiritual renewal.

This chapter has sought to articulate the close ties between the Sunday school and the growth of the Assemblies of God. Our Fellowship's Sunday school objectives have been used as a lens through which we can observe the power this 200-year-old movement has had on our Fellowship.

Some say it is a new day and with it must come new methods. Home Bible studies, lay Bible institutes, videotaped courses, and satellite linkage are the Sunday school of the 21st century. Let us welcome with open arms the new methodologies and ministries God is providing. They are not an enemy of the Sunday school, but complementary to its mission.

Renewing the Sunday School

We must remember, however, that this ministry has proven itself successful for over 200 years. The doomsday seers have prophesied Sunday school's demise since the beginning of the

19th century. The fact is, the Sunday school has staying power. If we understand its mission and do not expect more of it than it is meant to do, it will continue to serve our Movement. All the contemporary expressions of church education will be enhanced when working in harmony with the Sunday school as the hub.

Locke Bowman suggests six factors that are essential to the renewal of the entire Sunday school movement.[19]

1. *The leadership provided by clergy and professional Christian educators.* If church leaders decide the Sunday school needs renewing and empower the laity to devote talent and energy to the task, nothing can stop a renewal of Sunday school.

2. *The stress placed upon what it means to teach and learn.* The Sunday school, as a hub for evangelism and training for holy living, must continually train its teachers for the powerful ministry that the Sunday school class can provide.

3. *A fearless emphasis upon solid biblical scholarship.* Our pluralistic world calls for fearless and bold declaration of biblical truths that will provide the Assemblies of God with a membership that is not blown about by "every wind of doctrine" (Ephesians 4:14, KJV).

4. *An understanding of and accomplishment of the goals of the Sunday school.* We must understand the mission of the Assemblies of God Sunday school. Without a positive understanding of its mission and objectives it is doomed to stagnation.

5. *The rebuilding of widespread support structures to give Sunday school workers the vision and training necessary to maintain their commitment to the task.* Networking support structures need to flow beyond the professional Christian educator to the heart and soul of the Sunday school movement: the lay worker. Only when the laity know their mission and are equipped to better accomplish that task, will Sunday schools grow healthy. Lay workers must be reemphasized as those persons the sectional, district, and national offices seek to serve and support.

6. *A prayerful openness to the Holy Spirit's renewal.* We must realize that planning and praying are not antithetical. We can confidently await God's empowerment when we have planned structures for ministry that support and extend Christ's continued ministry on earth through the presence of His Spirit. If Sunday school can serve Christ's command that we disciple all nations and teach them to obey all that He has commanded, it can be expected that God will reign His blessing on those open to the moving of His Spirit.

The Assemblies of God has an enduring and rich Sunday school heritage. But we do not need a nostalgic return to the "glory years" of Sunday school. The ministry of reaching and teaching may take a number of forms, but the Sunday school will continue to prosper as "the Church—on one day, in one place, at one time, for at least one hour—studying God's Word."[20]

NOTES

[1]For a more liberal history see Robert W. Lynn and Elliott Wright, *The Big Little School* (Nashville, Tenn.: Abingdon Press, 1980.) For a more conservative history of the Sunday school see Wesley Willis, *200 Years and Still Counting* (Wheaton, Ill.: Victor Books, 1980); C.B. Eavey, *A Popular History of Christian Education* (Chicago: Moody Press, 1961).

[2]Willis, *200 Years and Still Counting,* p. 33.

[3]Edwin Wilbur Rice, *The Sunday School Movement, 1780–1917, and the American Sunday School Union, 1817–1917* (Philadelphia: The Union Press, 1917; reprint ed., Salem, N.H.: Ayer Company, Publishers, 1971).

[4]Eavey, *A Popular History of Christian Education.*

[5]Between 1926 and 1936, Assemblies of God Sunday schools showed a 300-percent increase in enrollment. See Stephen Rexroat, *The Sunday School Spirit* (Springfield, Mo.: Gospel Publishing House, 1979), p. 21.

[6]William Martin, *First Steps for Teachers* (Springfield, Mo.: Gospel Publishing House, 1984), p. 39.

[7]Ralph M. Riggs, *A Successful Pastor* (Springfield, Mo.: Gospel Publishing House, 1931), p. 96.

[8]Myer Pearlman, *Successful Sunday School Teaching* (Springfield, Mo.: Gospel Publishing House, 1935), p. 5.

[9]Martin, *First Steps for Teachers,* p. 42.

[10]Ibid., p. 43.

[11]Jack Seymour, "The Story of the Protestant Sunday School," *Renewing the Sunday School and the CCD,* ed. D. Campbell Wyckoff (Birmingham, Ala.: Religious Education Press, 1986), p. 25.

[12]Adapted from Billie Davis, *Teaching To Meet Crisis Needs* (Springfield, Mo.: Gospel Publishing House, 1984), pp. 17–19.

[13]David Torgerson, "The Assimilation Potential of Sunday School," *Sunday School Counselor,* September 1987.

[14]Billie Davis, interview with the Sunday School Department, Assemblies of God, Springfield, Missouri, 1984.

[15]Seymour, *Renewing the Sunday School and the CCD,* p. 10.

[16]Riggs, *A Successful Pastor,* p. 97.

[17]Howard Hendricks, *Teaching To Change Lives,* (Portland, Oreg.: Multnomah Publishing, 1987), pp. 9,10.

[18]David A. Moberg, *The Church as a Social Institution,* 2nd ed. (Grand Rapids: Baker Book House, 1984). Gary Burkhart, "Patterns of Protestant Organization," *American Denominational Organization: A Sociological View,* ed. Ross P. Scherer (Pasadena, Calif.: William Carey Library, 1980).

[19]Adapted from Locke E. Bowman, Jr., "Analysis and Assessment: The General Protestant Sunday School," *Renewing the Sunday School and the CCD,* pp. 110–112.

[20]A definition developed by Keith Heermann, director of Christian Education Ministries, Southern California District Council of the Assemblies of God.

3

The Person of the Holy Spirit

ANTHONY PALMA

Who, or what, is the Holy Spirit? The first-century church did not raise the question. But within a few centuries it became necessary for the Christian church to give attention to the matter. Some church leaders were teaching that the Holy Spirit was created by the Son of God and therefore could not be considered a member of the Godhead. This was actually a denial of the doctrine of the Trinity—that God exists eternally in three Persons whom we commonly designate as Father, Son, and Holy Spirit.

In this chapter we will deal with two main topics—the personality of the Holy Spirit and the deity of the Holy Spirit. This will be followed by a brief survey of early Church history as it relates to these matters.

The Personality of the Holy Spirit

The Scriptures clearly teach that the Holy Spirit is a personal being. Yet there is misunderstanding among some Christians on this matter, so that they refer to the Spirit as It rather than He.

Anthony Palma, Th.D. in New Testament, is administrator of Calvary Christian Academy, Philadelphia, Pennsylvania.

REASONS FOR THIS CONFUSION

Some of the main reasons for this misunderstanding include the following:

1. The Holy Spirit is the least mentioned of the three members of the Trinity. There are considerably more references in the Scriptures to the Father and to the Son than there are to the Holy Spirit. Consequently, less is known about Him than about the others.

2. The word *spirit* suggests an absence of personality. We have no difficulty in attaching the idea of personality to the words *father* and *son*. But in our language the word *spirit* is neuter in gender, which means the appropriate pronoun to be used is *it*. However, we will see that in spite of this accident of language there is abundant evidence in the Scriptures to prove the Holy Spirit is indeed a person.

3. The biblical languages are also partly responsible for this problem. Our word *spirit* is a simple and valid translation of the Hebrew *ruach* and the Greek *pneuma,* which are common words in those languages. Their basic meaning is that of wind, breath, or air. In the English language we have separate words for each of them. Hebrew and Greek can each use one word that has all those meanings.

Originally the words *ruach* and *pneuma* were used for inanimate and impersonal forces like wind and breath. Later, they were applied to what we understand by the word *spirit.* An interesting fact is that Hebrew has no neuter gender; its word for *spirit* is feminine in gender. In Greek, on the other hand, the word for *spirit* is neuter in gender. The point of all this is that both in the biblical languages and in English the doctrine of the Holy Spirit is sometimes misunderstood because of linguistic limitations.

4. Translations of the Bible are sometimes inadequate. This may be due to the translators' desire to give a "strict" translation, or to an unawareness of the overall biblical teaching about the Holy Spirit. For instance, Romans 8:26 in the King

James Version reads, "Likewise the Spirit also helpeth our infirmities: for we know not what we should pray for as we ought: but the Spirit *itself* maketh intercession for us with groanings which cannot be uttered." It is much better to follow the reading of the New American Standard Version, for instance, which says, ". . . the Spirit *Himself*. . . ."

5. The Holy Spirit is often associated in the Scriptures with the idea of power. Consequently some think of the Holy Spirit in terms of an impersonal force. But when Jesus promised the disciples they would receive power when the Holy Spirit came upon them (Luke 24:49; Acts 1:8), He meant that the Spirit himself would come in fullness and that the Spirit, who is all-powerful, would provide them with the necessary means for effective witnessing.

6. The figures of speech that are often used in the Scriptures for the Holy Spirit suggest the idea of inanimate or impersonal objects. Only a few suggestions are necessary to illustrate this point. He is likened to

Water—John 7:38,39
Oil—Acts 10:38 (Throughout the Bible anointing was done with oil.)
Wind—John 3:8; Acts 2:2
Fire—Acts 2:3,4
A dove—Luke 3:22

A figure of speech can be used to help us understand something about a person. If we say, "Pastor Jones is a real powerhouse for God," we do not mean that he is not a person. We are simply using an object from everyday life to express some characteristic or attribute of this person.

PROOF OF THE SPIRIT'S PERSONALITY

Many lines of evidence in the Scriptures point to the fact that the Holy Spirit is a Person and not an inanimate object or impersonal force. We can establish this by a survey of the biblical material.

1. He possesses personal attributes—qualities associated with the mind, the will, and the emotions.

Paul speaks of "the mind of the Spirit" (Romans 8:27) and says that only the Spirit of God knows "the deep things of God" (1 Corinthians 2:10,11). The Holy Spirit's intellectual activity is further seen in gifts of the Spirit such as a word of knowledge, a word of wisdom, discerning of spirits, and prophecy (1 Corinthians 12:8–10, KJV). Second, the Holy Spirit has a will, or volition. One aspect of this is His sovereignty. He distributes the gifts of the Spirit "to each one individually just as He wills" (1 Corinthians 12:11, NASB). He directs God's people in setting some apart for special ministry (Acts 13:2) and in the choice of fields of labor (Acts 16:6,7). Finally, the Holy Spirit has emotions. The Spirit may be grieved (Isaiah 63:10; Ephesians 4:30). He manifests love (Romans 15:30).

2. He performs personal acts. It will be sufficient simply to list some of these, with a few appropriate Scripture references:

He creates—Genesis 1:1,2; Job 33:4; Psalm 33:6.
He recreates, or regenerates—John 3:5; Titus 3:5.
He strives with men—Genesis 6:3 (KJV); Isaiah 63:10.
He convicts, or convinces, unregenerate men—John 16:8.
He intercedes—Romans 8:26.
He performs miracles—Acts 8:39; Hebrews 2:4.
He raises the dead—Romans 1:3,4; 8:11.
He speaks—John 16:13; Acts 8:29; 10:19; Revelation 2:7.
He teaches—Luke 12:12; John 14:26; 1 John 2:27.
He testifies—John 15:26; 1 Peter 1:11 (KJV).

3. He may be personally offended. Stephen charged his persecutors with always resisting the Holy Spirit (Acts 7:51). Peter accused Ananias of lying to the Holy Spirit (Acts 5:3) and further stated that both Ananias and Sapphira had put the Spirit of the Lord to the test (Acts 5:9). Paul admonishes Christians not to grieve the Holy Spirit (Ephesians 4:30), probably recalling how Israel had so offended Him in the wilderness (Isaiah 63:10). Furthermore, believers are warned of the possibility of

insulting or outraging "the Spirit of grace" by denying their blood-bought salvation (Hebrews 10:29). Then in one of the most solemn passages in all of Scripture, Jesus warns against blaspheming, or sinning against, the Holy Spirit (Matthew 12:22–32; Mark 3:22–30; Luke 12:10).

The precise nature of this sin is a subject of dispute among biblical scholars, but at least two points are quite clear when we examine the entire context: (1) It consists of *knowingly* and *persistently* attributing to Satan what is obviously the work of the Holy Spirit; and (2) it is a rejection of Jesus Christ as God's chosen and anointed One for the deliverance of mankind. No Christian need be preoccupied or distressed with the thought that he has committed this sin. The very fact that he is concerned about it is clear indication that the Holy Spirit has not forsaken him!

4. Jesus called Him the Paraclete. This term is a transliteration of the Greek *Paraklētos* and is translated variously as Comforter, Helper, Counselor, Advocate. Its root meaning is "one called to the side of." The passages where this title is found (John 14:16,26; 15:26; 16:7) clearly show that Jesus is talking about the Holy Spirit as a Person. As we noticed earlier, the New Testament writers were forced to use a neuter noun when they spoke of the Spirit because there was no other choice. But when there was a choice—as between neuter and masculine forms for *Paraclete*—they selected the masculine.

A further indication of the Spirit's personality is found in Jesus' words "another Paraclete" (John 14:16). Jesus himself was the first *Paraclete.* The apostle John tells us, "We have an advocate *[Paracletos]* with the Father, Jesus Christ the righteous" (1 John 2:1, KJV). The clue is in the word *another,* which in the Greek normally means "another of the same kind." Just as the Lord Jesus Christ comes to the aid of His people and encourages them, so the Holy Spirit likewise helps, encourages, and intercedes for those who belong to Him. Jesus promised He would not leave His disciples as orphans—helpless, defenseless, comfortless (John 14:18).

Masculine pronouns are used for the Holy Spirit. It seems that in a few passages Jesus deliberately emphasized the personality of the Spirit by using the masculine form of a pronoun when He could have omitted the pronoun (as in John 14:26 [NASB] where the word *He* could have been omitted without injury to the grammar) or where He could have used a neuter form (as in John 16:13,14, where the neuter word *Spirit* is found).

The Deity of the Holy Spirit

The Holy Spirit is a member of the Trinity, which means He is fully divine like the Father and the Son. Following our discussion in the preceding section of this chapter, we may now confidently call Him the Third Person of the Godhead.

SCRIPTURAL EVIDENCE FOR HIS DEITY

Many lines of evidence prove the Holy Spirit as absolute deity. The most important ones are the following:

1. He is mentioned coordinately with the Father and the Son. The following examples demonstrate that all three are coequal. Otherwise it would be a case of mixing the proverbial apples and oranges!

Jesus commanded the disciples to baptize believers "in the name of the Father and the Son and the Holy Spirit" (Matthew 28:19, NASB).

Paul, in three parallel phrases, speaks of "the grace of the Lord Jesus Christ, and the love of God, and the fellowship of the Holy Spirit" (2 Corinthians 13:14). In Ephesians 4:4–6 he speaks of one Lord, one Spirit, one God and Father.

2. The Spirit is clearly distinguished from the Father and the Son. He must not be regarded simply as a manifestation of God, as though He did not have a separate identity. The prophet Isaiah quotes the Messiah as saying, "The Lord God, and his Spirit, hath sent me" (48:16, KJV). This distinction of identities is also evident at the baptism of Jesus. The Son of God was standing in the Jordan River, the Holy Spirit came

upon Him in the form of a dove, and the Father spoke from heaven (Luke 3:21,22).

In the Bible the Holy Spirit is often called the Spirit of God, or the Spirit of the Lord. Because of this, some have concluded that He does not have independent existence and must be regarded simply as a manifestation of God. However, such titles are used to emphasize that the Spirit is divine and not evil. Many evil, satanic spirits are at work in our world, but there is only one divine Holy Spirit. The tripersonality of the Godhead must be maintained; otherwise, it is impossible to come to a satisfactory understanding of some passages of Scripture.

3. He has divine attributes. Divine attributes are characteristics or qualities that God alone possesses. Among the most important are the following:

Eternality. God alone has neither beginning nor ending. Hebrews 9:14 describes the Holy Spirit as "the eternal Spirit."

Omnipotence. The Holy Spirit is all-powerful. This is evident throughout the Scriptures by the mighty signs and wonders that are wrought by Him (Romans 15:19; Hebrews 2:4). He participated in the creation of our world (Genesis 1:1,2). He effects the new creation, or the new birth (John 3:5; Titus 3:5). He raises the dead (Romans 1:3,4; 8:11).

Omnipresence. He is everywhere present. David said, "Where can I go from your Spirit? Where can I flee from your presence?" (Psalm 139:7). The answer is an obvious nowhere! Difficult as it is for the human, finite mind to comprehend, the Spirit of God is simultaneously present everywhere. How else would it be possible for Christians everywhere to be engaged in worship at the same time, inasmuch as worship is possible only by means of the Holy Spirit (John 4:23,24; Philippians 3:3)?

Omniscience. The Holy Spirit is all-knowing. Nothing is hidden from Him (1 Corinthians 2:10,11). As the One who inspired the Holy Scriptures, He revealed to Moses details of the creation story that would be otherwise unknowable to man. By the operation of gifts of the Spirit, such as prophecy and a word of knowledge, He discloses inner secrets and sins of men's hearts

(1 Corinthians 14:24,25). He guides God's people into all truth (John 16:13) and gives them spiritual insight (1 Corinthians 2:9,10).

Not only is the Holy Spirit omniscient in matters pertaining to the eternal past and the present; He also knows all about the future. It was He who moved upon the biblical writers to record events of the last days, for Jesus said the Spirit would show His disciples "things to come" (John 16:13, KJV). And Paul records, "The Spirit clearly says that in later times some will abandon the faith and follow deceiving spirits and things taught by demons" (1 Timothy 4:1).

Absolute holiness. The designation *Holy Spirit* occurs more than 90 times in Scripture; all but three references are found in the New Testament. He is specifically called *the* Holy Spirit, indicating His unique holiness and also His separateness from all other spirit-beings, such as Satan, evil spirits, and angels. Paul goes so far as to call Him "the Spirit of holiness" (Romans 1:4), which is really the way the title "Holy Spirit" is expressed in the Hebrew language (Psalm 51:11; Isaiah 63:10,11).

4. He performs the works of Deity. God alone can create and sustain our universe. He alone can regenerate and spiritually resurrect souls that are dead in trespasses and sin. He alone has power to raise people from the dead. Yet, as we previously noted, the Holy Spirit either participates in or is the sole agent of these works.

5. He is expressly called God. The apostle Peter accepted without question the full deity of the Holy Spirit. This is especially evident in his encounter with Ananias and Sapphira (Acts 5:1–11). Peter said to Ananias, "Why has Satan filled your heart to lie to the Holy Spirit?" (v. 3, NASB). Then in the following verse he says, "You have not lied to men, but to God" (NASB). When one sins against the Holy Spirit he is sinning against God.

PRAYER AND PRAISE TO THE HOLY SPIRIT

Is it proper to pray to the Holy Spirit, or to ascribe praise to

Him? This is a natural question to raise now that we have established both His personality and His deity. We have already seen that He is coequal with the Father and the Son. But there is no clear indication in the Scriptures that He may be addressed in prayer or in worship. Prayer is normally made to the Father through Jesus our Mediator, and it is done in or by the Holy Spirit (John 4:23,24; Philippians 3:3).

Two prayers in the New Testament indirectly invoke the Holy Spirit. At the conclusion of 2 Corinthians Paul asks that the fellowship of the Holy Spirit may be with the Corinthian Christians (13:14). John, in the Book of Revelation, asks that grace and peace may come to his readers "from the seven Spirits who are before His [God's] throne" (1:4, NASB). The seven Spirits are elsewhere called the seven Spirits of God (3:1; 4:5; 5:6). This is an obvious reference to the Holy Spirit, even though the number seven may confuse some. The Book of Revelation contains much symbolism, and numbers in this book are often symbolic. Seven is the number of completeness; therefore, "seven Spirits" refers to the Spirit of God in His fullness or His complete activity.

Isaiah 11:2,3 is often taken as an explanation of this inasmuch as it contains seven small commentaries on the Holy Spirit: "The Spirit *of the Lord* will rest on him [the Messiah]— the Spirit *of wisdom* and of *understanding,* the Spirit *of counsel* and *of power,* the Spirit *of knowledge* and *of the fear of the Lord.*"

In Revelation 4:6–9, four angelic beings around the throne of God worship Him, saying, "Holy, holy, holy, is the Lord God Almighty" (v. 8). They are similar to the seraphim in Isaiah's vision who say to one another, "Holy, holy, holy, is the Lord of hosts" (Isaiah 6:3, NASB). Some biblical scholars take this triple repetition of the word *holy* to be an ascription of praise to each member of the Trinity.

Although there is no clear example in the Scriptures of prayer or praise addressed to the Spirit, there is nothing that prohibits it. And it is perfectly natural for one who believes the Holy

Spirit to be God to pray to Him occasionally. This is reflected especially in hymns and choruses. Not only do we sing *about* the Holy Spirit, but we also sing *to* Him in hymns like "Holy Spirit, Faithful Guide"; "Holy Ghost, With Light Divine"; and "Breathe on Me, Breath of God"; and in choruses like "Spirit of the Living God" and "Come, Holy Spirit, I Need Thee."

The Creeds of the Early Church

One church historian has defined a creed as "a statement of faith for public use; it contains articles needful for salvation and the theological well-being of the Church." We may think of it more simply as a statement of the church's beliefs written down so that Christians may be able to distinguish between false doctrine and true doctrine.

During the first century no formal creed was adopted by the church. But as time went on, false teachings increasingly made their appearance. Consequently there emerged three great creeds that articulated what the church considered to be sound doctrine. Our concern is to see what each of these says about the Holy Spirit.

THE APOSTLES' CREED

Contrary to what its name suggests, this was not a creed drawn up by the apostles. Its exact date cannot be fixed with certainty but very possibly it emerged during the second century. It received this title because it was believed to reflect the teaching of the apostles.

This creed contains only two references to the Spirit. In the section about Jesus Christ, it says that He "was conceived by the Holy Spirit." Following that section it says simply, "I believe . . . in the Holy Spirit." It was not until a controversy arose about the personality and deity of the Holy Spirit that we find some additional statements about Him in the next great creed.

THE NICENE CREED

The Council of Nicea in A.D. 325 drew up a creed that amplified the Apostles' Creed but added nothing concerning the Holy Spirit. In A.D. 381 the Council of Constantinople expanded the Nicene Creed and, because of controversy over the Holy Spirit, included some details about His nature and work.

The heresy of Arianism denied the deity of both the Son and the Holy Spirit. Macedonius, bishop of Constantinople from A.D. 341 to 360, was especially prominent among those denying the Spirit's deity. He taught that the Holy Spirit was inferior and subordinate to both the Father and the Son, and spoke of Him as a messenger or minister. In effect, he said that the Spirit was on the same level as angels, who are God's messengers. The Spirit was thus reduced to the status of a creature. The followers of Macedonius, who were often called Macedonians or Pneumatomachians (literally, "Spirit-fighters"), taught that the Father created the Son and the Son in turn created the Holy Spirit. Therefore, a created being—a creature—could not be God.

This creed, which more properly should be called the Niceno-Constantinopolitan Creed, clearly stated the personality and deity of the Spirit in the following article: "And [I believe] in the Holy Spirit, the Lord and Giver of life, who proceeds from the Father, who with the Father and the Son is worshiped and glorified together; who spoke by the prophets."

In A.D. 451, at the Council of Chalcedon, the Church in the western part of the Roman Empire also adopted this creed.

THE ATHANASIAN CREED

The origin of this creed is unknown, but the name of the church father Augustine is associated with it. It came into existence prior to the fifth century. It is so called because it reflects the theology of another important church father, Athanasius. Although not composed by him, it sets forth much of his argumentation in favor of the doctrine of the Trinity.

Listed below are excerpts from this creed. The language may seem unnecessarily repetitious, but in an era when the heresy of Arianism threatened to displace the doctrine of the Trinity, it was necessary to be explicit.

> There is one Godhead of the Father and of the Son and of the Holy Spirit, equal in glory and coequal in majesty.
>
> The Father is uncreated, the Son is uncreated, the Holy Spirit is uncreated.
>
> The Father is unlimited, the Son is unlimited, the Holy Spirit is unlimited.
>
> The Father is eternal, the Son is eternal, the Holy Spirit is eternal.
>
> The Father is almighty, the Son is almighty, the Holy Spirit is almighty; and yet there are not three who are almighty but there is one who is almighty.
>
> So the Father is God, the Son is God, the Holy Spirit is God, and yet they are not three Gods but one God.
>
> So the Father is Lord, the Son is Lord, the Holy Spirit is Lord, and yet they are not three Lords but one Lord.
>
> The Holy Spirit was not made or created or begotten, but proceeds from the Father and Son.

As we have seen in this chapter, both the Scriptures and the Early Church taught that the Holy Spirit is not an impersonal force but rather the Third Person of the Trinity with all the attributes of the Godhead.

4

The Holy Spirit and the Word

EDGAR LEE

The Holy Spirit is the Person of the Godhead most distinctively involved with the writing of the Bible, the Word of God. Peter gives a graphic look at the Spirit's work when he observes, "No prophecy of Scripture came about by the prophet's own interpretation. For prophecy never had its origin in the will of man, but *men spoke from God* as they were *carried along by the Holy Spirit*" (2 Peter 1:20,21, emphasis added). This careful translation of the original Greek clearly shows that God has been able to communicate His will through men in dynamic encounters with His Spirit.

Revelation

There is a definite direction in the communications process that gave us the Word of God. It is from God to man and never from man to God. Peter denied following "cleverly invented stories" created by man (2 Peter 1:16). He also went to great pains to show that man was not responsible for the content of the Scriptures. The Source of the message is always God himself. Man is clearly a partner in the process, but he did not determine the content or its timing and manner of impartation.

Edgar Lee, S.T.D., is vice president for academic affairs at Southeastern College of the Assemblies of God, Lakeland, Florida.

There are several basic reasons for the God-to-man direction of the communications process. One is the creatureliness of man. Although God created man "very good" (Genesis 1:31) and capable of fellowship with Him when He came to the Garden of Eden in "the cool of the day" (Genesis 3:8), man was always creature rather than Creator. Man never initiated—nor indeed could do so—the spiritual and intellectual fellowship he originally experienced with God.

To the limitations of creatureliness, Adam and Eve soon added a second reason, their personal sin, as the subtle suggestions of the serpent tempted them to eat the forbidden fruit (Genesis 3:6) and culminated in their being driven from the Garden (Genesis 3:23,24). Paul reported on the awful consequences in the New Testament, "The result of one trespass was condemnation for all men" (Romans 5:18). All men became sinners (Romans 3:23) and found themselves incapable of truly understanding God (Ephesians 4:18).

The third reason is that the Creator whom man has rejected is utterly transcendent to man. Absolutely perfect in power, knowledge, and righteousness, God in His essential being is absolutely beyond the reach of fallen man. Job's friend, Elihu, confessed, "The Almighty is beyond our reach" (Job 37:23). Isaiah cried, "Who has understood the Spirit of the Lord, or instructed him as his counselor?" (40:13). Overwhelmed with God's glory, Paul noted that God "lives in unapproachable light" and "no one has seen or can see [Him]" (1 Timothy 6:16).

So man, whose very fashioning was an act of divine love and condescension, rejected his always glorious and transcendent Creator and broke the line of communication that God had opened when man was first formed. Man could then do nothing himself to reestablish that contact.

Incredibly, however, the rejected Creator still loved His fallen creature. Love is, in fact, intrinsic to God's very nature (1 John 4:16). In His great mercy, God began a long, careful plan to reopen communications with man and redeem him. Unfolding slowly over the centuries, it led through Seth, Noah, and Abraham and the Patriarchs with whom God established a covenant. It included Moses who led the Israelites out of Egypt and gave them God's law. Joshua and Samuel, David and Solomon, Isaiah and Malachi, and all their fellow servants were instrumental in working out and telling about God's plan of redemption. Finally, it was completed in the crucified and resurrected Christ who has poured out His Spirit, is building His church, and is preparing for His return and the glorification of His saints.

So God himself designed a plan of redemption, carried it out, and explained himself to feeble man in the Bible. This divine disclosure is called "revelation." God chose to have the Holy Spirit bring it through men who recorded it for us on the pages of the Bible.

A Divine Book

While Peter clearly understood that the Bible had its origin in God, it may be readily demonstrated that this is also the teaching of the entire Bible. A classic passage from Paul's writings gives us vital insight into the divine nature of the Scriptures: "All Scripture is *God-breathed* and is useful for teaching, rebuking, correcting and training in righteousness" (2 Timothy 3:16, emphasis added). "God-breathed" is an accurate translation of *theopneustos,* a term used only once in the Greek New Testament. Coined from *theos,* meaning "God," and *pneo,* meaning "to blow, breathe," the term is richly suggestive of the ministry of the Spirit, whose Greek name is *pneuma.* Clearly, Paul's understanding is that the presence and power of God pervade the Bible and constitute it a divine Book. He calls the Old Testament "the holy Scriptures" (2 Timothy 3:15).

The Bible's nature as a divine Book may be demonstrated in several other ways by a quick survey of the Old and New Testaments. So important are the Ten Commandments—the heart of the Old Testament law—for example, that God himself wrote them on tablets of stone and gave them to Moses (Exodus 31:18).

When Moses, angered and grieved by Israel's sin, broke the first tablets, God wrote them a second time (34:1). Note also how God, speaking uniquely to Moses in a very direct way that sounds much like modern dictation, gave him instructions on the construction of the tabernacle (Exodus 25 to 27) as well as the specific laws Israel was to observe.

God was so involved with Isaiah that He actually does appear to have dictated at least one brief message, telling the prophet, "Take a large scroll and write on it with an ordinary pen: Maher-Shalal-Hash-Baz" (Isaiah 8:1). The point is not that God dictated all Scripture. The most casual reading of the Bible will show that to be untrue. What is being traced is the divine initiative present in the biblical understanding of the giving of the Scriptures.

Some additional evidences of God's initiative may be noted in the following brief survey of the Bible which, of course, could be expanded many times over: In psalm, David cried out, "The Spirit of the Lord spoke through me; his word was on my tongue" (2 Samuel 23:2). "The Lord Almighty has spoken," declared Micah (4:4). "This is what the Lord says," asserted Amos (1:3). God told Habakkuk to "write down the revelation and make it plain on tablets" (2:2). Over and over, the prophets report that "the word of the Lord" came to them (Hosea 1:1; Joel 1:1; Jonah 1:1; Zephaniah 1:1). Thus the Old Testament writers clearly understood themselves to be speaking and writing under divine impulse.

There was a renewed outbreak of Spirit-inspired prophetic activity with the beginning of the New Testament era. Elizabeth, by the Spirit, blessed Mary who responded in equally inspired terms (Luke 1:41–55). Zechariah was filled with the Spirit to prophesy of the coming salvation in Christ for whom his son, John the Baptist, would be the forerunner (Luke 1:67–79). Even the characteristic Old Testament prophetic formula reappears in the ministry of the Baptist: "The word of God came to John" (Luke 3:2), and with that event, John began his public ministry.

Jesus clearly understood himself to be anointed by the Spirit to preach His message. In Luke's Gospel Jesus' sermon in the Nazareth synagogue is at the forefront, explaining the significance of His ministry: "The Spirit of the Lord is on me, because he has anointed me to preach good news to the poor" (4:18). The Gospel writers understood Jesus to be the Son of God but they remembered and noted His dependence on the Holy Spirit in His incarnate life.

Putting the divine initiative another way, John's Gospel shows that Jesus came to make God known: "No one has ever seen God, but God the only Son who is at the Father's side, has made him known" (1:18). In His high priestly prayer, speaking of His disciples, Jesus told His Father, "I gave them the words you gave me and they accepted them" (John 17:8). Once again, there is a strong awareness that it is the divine message which is presented.

With the death and resurrection of Jesus and the outpouring of the Holy Spirit, the prophetic mantle fell upon the apostles. Peter's Pentecost sermon is really a prophetic address, as the unusual term *apophtheggomai* (translated "raised his voice") in Acts 2:14 attests. Paul was confident that "in the gospel a righteousness from God is revealed" (Romans 1:17). He rejoiced with the Thessalonians that the word of God had not been heard as the word of men but, indeed, as the very word of God (1 Thessalonians 2:13).

In Revelation, the last book of the New Testament, John, "in the Spirit," received orders to "write . . . what you see," and obeyed as the eschatological message began to unfold (1:10,11). The writer to the Hebrews drew the New Testament revelatory activity of God to a fine focus in the Lord Jesus Christ:

> In the past God spoke to our forefathers through the prophets at many times and in various ways, but in these last days he has spoken to us by his Son, whom he appointed heir of all things, and through whom he made the universe. The Son is the radiance of God's glory and the exact representation of his being, sustaining all things by his powerful word (1:1–3).

What this quick overview demonstrates is that those whose messages came to be deposited in the sacred canon of Scripture had a very strong consciousness that they were indeed moved by the Holy Spirit to speak from God. The Bible purports throughout to be the very Word of God and only on those terms can it be the basis of all Christian preaching and teaching.

A Human Book

It is also important that the Bible be understood as a human book. "Men spoke from God" and it was men who "were carried along by the Holy Spirit" (2 Peter 1:21). While the foregoing panoramic tour of the biblical landscape focused on the divine side of the biblical message, it has at the same time demonstrated quite well that the All-Wise chose to make human beings His partners in receiving, sharing, and recording His messages. It is possible to be so zealous in lifting up the divine side of Scripture that the human side of its production is suppressed.

If one is to do justice to what the Spirit has done in the preparation of the Bible, he must note the way the Spirit uses persons in the process. Every human contributor to the Bible has a uniquely personal style and his contribution is frequently colored by his personal experience. God certainly did not dictate the Bible word by word in a standard, unvarying language. He poured His message through fully conscious, cooperative, marvelously diverse, and talented humans.

The Scriptures contain poetry which, for example, powerfully expresses the suffering of Job. But prose is predominant in both Testaments. Included also are David's psalms crying for deliverance as he was hounded by Saul, Solomon's proverbs with godly advice for life, and Isaiah's exalted vision of God. Amos, the uneducated shepherd of Tekoa, uses agrarian imagery and some of the finest Hebrew in the Old Testament to describe his visions. Long genealogies are found in Genesis and, especially, 1 Chronicles.

Moving to the New Testament, one discovers the Gospels, a

brand-new literary genre that came into being to tell the story of Jesus. Paul and his fellow apostles took the common letter form of the day and used it to set forth the theology and ethics of Christianity under the direction of the Spirit of God. But each Gospel writer is unique and each letter writer is different in style and interests.

Human research is not inconsistent with the preparation of Scripture, either. Luke prefaced his Gospel (the Gospel of Luke and the Acts of the Apostles seem to have been originally one volume) with this statement: "I myself have carefully investigated everything from the beginning" (Luke 1:3). Even uninspired sources were used in the biblical record, for instance, the Book of Jashar (2 Samuel 1:18), the annals of Solomon (1 Kings 11:41), the annals of the kings of Judah (1 Kings 14:29), the records of Samuel and of Nathan (1 Chronicles 29:29), the records of Shemaiah and Iddo (2 Chronicles 12:15), and the annotations on the book of the kings (2 Chronicles 24:27).

Unlikely sources are sometimes cited, such as Paul's quoting a pagan poet to his Athenian listeners, " 'We are his offspring' " (Acts 17:28). Jude refers to apocryphal literature in mentioning the prophecy of "Enoch, the seventh from Adam" (Jude 14).

All of these marvelously diverse human contributors were meticulously prepared by divine providence for their unique roles. Several examples may be highlighted: In the case of Moses, the hand of God is quickly seen as the baby becomes a refugee from Pharaoh's infanticide and is found floating in the reeds along the Nile by Pharaoh's own daughter who raises him at court as her son (Exodus 2:1–10). Stephen reported that "Moses was educated in all the wisdom of the Egyptians" (Acts 7:22), which Moses' adoption by the royal family would imply. While Moses would receive quite another education as a shepherd in the deserts of Sinai, this Egyptian schooling, so rare in the ancient world, would enable him to write God's law which was absolutely essential for the emerging nation of Israel.

Once again we cite Stephen's history of Moses with interest: "He was in the congregation in the desert, with . . . the angel who spoke to him on Mount Sinai; and he received living words to pass on to us" (Acts 7:38). Moses is a perfect illustration of an imperfect man providentially prepared to write Scripture.

Jeremiah is another example of providential preparation. Note the development of the dialogue in his call to prophetic office recorded in Jeremiah 1:4–9:

JEREMIAH: "The word of the Lord came to me saying, . . ."
GOD: " 'Before I formed you in the womb I knew you, before you were born I set you apart; I appointed you as a prophet to the nations.' "
JEREMIAH: " 'I do not know how to speak.' "
GOD: " 'I have put my words in your mouth.' "

Here is God's testimony that Jeremiah was prepared from his conception to serve as a prophet. Then the time also came when the Spirit of God decisively came upon him for ministry— a prepared vessel filled with a mighty anointing! Even a casual reading of Jeremiah's book makes it clear that the words God put in his mouth were filtered through Jeremiah's unique personality and preparation.

Paul is a New Testament example of preparation for the writing of Scripture. His Jeremiah-like sense of destiny may be noted in the following passage: "God, who set me apart from birth and called me by his grace, was pleased to reveal his Son in me so that I might preach him among the Gentiles" (Galatians 1:15).

Paul's growth and education were almost as striking as that of Moses. He proudly testified to being born in Tarsus of Cilicia, raised in Jerusalem the center of Jewry, and trained under the leading rabbi of his time, Gamaliel (Acts 22:3).

Doctrine of Inspiration

Based on the biblical evidence, a sound doctrine of inspiration consisting of a definition and several qualifications can now be attempted. Inspiration may be defined as the supernatural guidance of the Holy Spirit which enabled the writers of Scrip-

ture to express God's revelation to man in a completely trustworthy way that also reflected their unique personalities.

Inspiration is *plenary,* meaning "full, entire, complete." The
whole Bible is inspired, the Old Testament as well as the New;
poetry as well as prose; genealogies and records as well as
exciting narratives. Every single part of every book is God-
breathed.

Inspiration is also *verbal,* indicating that each Hebrew, Ar-
amaic, and Greek word of the original manuscripts is exactly
the word God wished to use to express His revelation. Not a
single word is careless, accidental, or meaningless. This voids
any notion that inspiration relates only to ideas or concepts,
with specific words being a matter of indifference.

Scripture, being inspired, is *infallible* and *inerrant.* Both
terms mean much the same with Webster defining the first
"not fallible, not capable of error, never wrong" and the second
"not erring, making no mistake, infallible." But since *infallible*
seems to have lost precision in modern theological debate, de-
fenders of historic scriptural infallibility have moved to the use
and defense of *inerrancy.*

Inerrancy maintains that everything affirmed in the original manuscripts of Scripture is without error, whether it concerns faith and practice (doctrine and ethics) or history and
science. If the Bible teaches or records something, it is true.

The Bible is not, however, intended to be a textbook on science and should not be understood as such. One also recognizes
that, while modern scientific study has in large measure val-
idated the truth of the Bible, there are still a few unsolved
questions in the biblical text as it stands today, having been
handed down through the centuries. The original manuscripts,
of course, deteriorated long ago and are not available. Very
plausible explanations exist for most of these questions, and
the believer is confident that when all the facts are in the
accuracy of the biblical text will be absolutely established.

Those who are inclined to attribute error to Scripture should
note again the statements of the Lord Jesus who placed great

confidence, not just in every word, but in every letter of the Old Testament: "I tell you the truth, until heaven and earth disappear, not the smallest letter, not the least stroke of a pen, will by any means disappear from the Law until everything is accomplished" (Matthew 5:18). Jesus spoke similarly regarding His own words: "Heaven and earth will pass away, but my words will never pass away" (Matthew 24:35). John's Gospel records His absolute affirmation, "The Scripture cannot be broken" (10:35). It certainly seems that following Jesus requires a belief in the Bible's theological and scientific inerrancy.

It should be remembered that the doctrine of inspiration has to do with the writing of Scripture only. It does not guarantee prophetic utterances, of whatever origin, that are not contained in the biblical canon of 66 books affirmed by the Spirit to the Church as God's Word. If an utterance is not written in the Bible, it is not inspired in the same sense as Scripture.

It should be remembered too that while all of Scripture is *inspired,* not all of Scripture is equally *inspiring.* Temple liturgy, genealogies, census lists, and so on are not always obviously edifying. It is the function of inspiration to assure that information is accurately recorded in keeping with the full-orbed divine purpose which is not always apparent to believing men and women. Inspiration does not guarantee that all information is exciting.

Yet another qualification is that the doctrine of inspiration ensures only that each statement or action is accurately recorded. It does not guarantee the theological or ethical correctness of the words and deeds of sinning persons. One does not imitate David's adultery or Peter's denial. Good hermeneutics, or interpretation, looks to the larger context of the individual book and the Bible as a whole to arrive at God's verdict on particular events, or statements, that may be recorded.

Authority

A divinely inspired record of God's communication to man

must, of necessity, be pervaded with authority and so the Bible claims to be. The apostolic lessons on inspiration were set within a context of concern for spiritual authority.

Paul admonished Timothy to continue in what he had learned and become convinced of from the Old Testament Scriptures and the apostolic proclamation (2 Timothy 3:14,15). The Scriptures, now complete in both testaments, are God-breathed and are "useful for teaching, rebuking, correcting and training in righteousness" (v. 16).

Peter challenged his readers to "be all the more eager to make your calling and election sure" (2 Peter 1:10). Then he added, "We have the word of the prophets made more certain, and you will do well to pay attention to it" (1:19). God-breathed Scripture written by those carried along by the Holy Spirit was the unvarying source of authority to which these apostles pointed.

In so doing, the apostles faithfully followed in the steps of their Lord who, himself, had always found clear and unvarying guidance in the words of Scripture for His own life and ministry. Jesus' rock-hard confidence in the accuracy and permanence of the Old Testament has already been noted in treating inerrancy. In some of His final sayings in Luke's Gospel, Jesus chided the Emmaus pair for being "slow of heart to believe all that the prophets have spoken" (Luke 24:25), and then proceeded to give them a lesson on what all the Scriptures said about himself. Meeting thereafter with the Eleven, Jesus went through much the same dialogue:

> This is what I told you while I was still with you: Everything must be fulfilled that is written about me in the Law of Moses, the Prophets and the Psalms. Then he opened their minds so they could understand the Scriptures (Luke 24:44,45).

The Holy Spirit would shortly be outpoured and He would provide very important guidance for the emerging Church and eventuate the completion of the Scriptures of the New Testament. But never did the Spirit lead the Church to depart from its definitive authority, the Scriptures.

The authority question is still with mankind and indeed is more acute than ever in the modern era which has seen the breakdown of traditional Judeo–Christian beliefs, the rise of countless competing philosophies and life-styles, and a pervasive unwillingness to commit to any absolutes.

Unlike other moderns who may find their authority in a particular religious or philosophical tradition, or in a notoriously subjective and shifting human reason, the Bible-believing Christian must always find ultimate authority in the Scriptures. Nor is the interest so much in the Bible as a book (though it is surely a book), but in the Bible as the guaranteed record of the disclosure of God's nature and His purposes and directions for man. As such, what the Bible says, God says. It has absolute right to determine one's beliefs and practices on all matters it touches, regardless of man's feelings to the contrary. The Bible rightly understood must always be used to correct man's ideas; man's ideas do not correct the Bible.

It cannot be overemphasized in the modern religious context that every person, every church, every ministry, every life-style, even every spiritual utterance in a worship service, must be judged and corrected by the Word of God.

Finally, the message of the Bible can never be separated from the Living God whose word it is. The paper or print may deteriorate or be destroyed but the message is eternal and eternally purposive. How apt the words of Isaiah 55:10,11:

> As the rain and the snow come down from heaven, and do not return to it without watering the earth and making it bud and flourish, so that it yields seed for the sower and bread for the eater, so is my word that goes out from my mouth: It will not return to me empty, but will accomplish what I desire and achieve the purpose for which I sent it.

5

The Holy Spirit and Illumination

EDGAR LEE

Although God's revelation in the Bible has been completed by the inspiring power of the Holy Spirit working through godly men, a continuing ministry of the Spirit is needed to enable the Word to effect its mission in the hearts of men and the life of the church.

This further ministry is called *illumination,* the process by which the Holy Spirit enables the believer to understand the Scriptures so its truth may be experienced and applied in daily life and faith. Illumination occurs in the interaction of the Holy Spirit and the Bible, as the written Word of God, in the consciousness of the believer.

At the beginning of any study of illumination it is important to examine each of these two great resources for knowing God's will.

The Spirit of Truth

"Let God be true, and every man a liar," wrote Paul, insisting on the integrity of God (Romans 3:4). God is supremely a God of truth; He cannot lie. This attribute of God is usually expressed in the Old Testament as *faithfulness,* or *steadfastness,* but occasionally God is spoken of as the "God of truth" (Isaiah 65:16). God always is exactly as He has revealed himself to be in the Bible, and He never fails to keep His word.

Not surprisingly, Jesus, the incarnate Son of God, spoke of himself in much the same terms. "I am the way and the truth and the life," He said (John 14:6). John the Baptist testified, "Grace and truth came through Jesus Christ" (John 1:17). The introduction of the letter to Philadelphia in the Revelation of John describes the risen Christ as He "who is holy and true" (Revelation 3:7).

Jesus very pointedly introduced the Holy Spirit to His disciples as "the Spirit of truth" (John 14:16,17; 15:26; 16:13). There can be little doubt that truth is of the very essence of the Godhead, inherent in the nature of the Father, Son, and Spirit. God must always be faithful to His nature and His Word. As He comes into contact with the believer through the Spirit, the believer has within himself a powerful force tending toward truth. Nothing false can emanate from the divine presence. The Spirit always resists a lie while reinforcing the truth.

Jesus' promise to the Twelve is to be understood in that light: "The Spirit of truth . . . will guide you into all truth" (John 16:13). The Spirit's role as guide is a very significant one, for Jesus also taught, "The Counselor . . . will teach you all things and will remind you of everything I have said to you" (14:26). Undoubtedly, this promise refers to the function of the Spirit in helping the apostles with their unique authoritative teaching role in the Apostolic Church, including the writing of the Gospels and Epistles.

That the promise also applies significantly to the Church at large may be seen in the fact that the Spirit carries out this role among ordinary believers in the New Testament churches. Thus Paul remarks to the Thessalonians, "Our gospel came to you not simply with words, but also with power, with the Holy Spirit and with deep conviction" (1 Thessalonians 1:5). The Spirit of truth was at work among those new Christians to impart, and attest the validity of, the message of the gospel. He continues in the modern era to lead sincere men and women of faith to an ever-expanding knowledge of God and His Word.

The Canon

The second great resource in the personal experience of the

Christian believer is the Bible. Here one needs to be even more specific by delimiting the Bible to the established canon of 66 books: 39 in the Old Testament and 27 in the New Testament. The Old Testament canon (which never included the books of the Apocrypha) seems to have been recognized by the Old Testament community. The Spirit also guided the early Christian church to recognize the 27 truly God-breathed books of the New Testament. Not only did the Spirit inspire the writing of these books, but also their collection and preservation. It is this biblical canon—and nothing else—that constitutes the objective authority for the church of the Lord Jesus Christ.

Here too the Church follows the example of her Lord. Jesus clearly had great reverence for the Old Testament canon of Scripture. He came not "to abolish the Law or the Prophets; . . . but to fulfill them" (Matthew 5:17). While Jesus' teachings often went beyond the Old Testament and formed the core of the New Testament canon, they never changed or contradicted the older covenant on which they were squarely founded.

The apostles too had the same respect for the Old Testament canon. They were thoroughly versed in it, read it, quoted from it, and saw Jesus and the Church as the fulfillment of it. One of Paul's last written instructions to Timothy was "bring . . . my scrolls, especially the parchments," quite likely referring to the Old Testament (2 Timothy 4:13).

Not until the fourth century did the church complete the task of clarifying the New Testament canon as far as every single book was concerned. However, there never was any real doubt about the canonicity of the major books. The process of canonization was well underway during the lifetime of the apostles. Peter, in his teachings about authority and certainty, grouped Paul's letters with "the other Scriptures" (2 Peter 3:16).

Note how carefully the apostles taught and guarded the authoritative message they had been given. Nothing other than the divine Word could claim authority over their lives. To the Corinthians, who were struggling with the claims of a small group that Christ had not risen, Paul wrote, "What I received

I passed on to you as of first importance: that Christ died for our sins *according to the Scriptures,* that he was buried, that he was raised on the third day *according to the Scriptures"* (1 Corinthians 15:3, emphasis added). These are the unshakable fundamentals of the gospel.

To the Galatians, who were being hounded by Judaizers insisting on salvation through the keeping of the Law, Paul thundered, "Even if we or an angel from heaven should preach a gospel other than the one we preached to you, let him be eternally condemned!" (Galatians 1:8). What an affirmation of the Word! Not even an angel could change it.

The Christian may be assured that the Spirit has inspired the Scriptures and that process is now complete. Having spoken, He will bring no new revelation altering or enlarging that which is given. He will lead man into fuller understanding, but it will be an elucidation of what He has already said. The Bible is the eternal, unchanging foundation for faith and life. It is the once-given word of God himself.

Illumination and the Believer

Man does not naturally receive the truths of God, hence the need for personal illumination. Paul vividly depicted the darkness of the human heart when he said, "The god of this age has blinded the minds of unbelievers, so that they cannot see the light of the gospel of the glory of Christ" (2 Corinthians 4:4). The work of the Holy Spirit can, however, alter that grim spiritual reality. Paul went on to say, "God . . . made his light shine in our hearts to give us the light of the knowledge of the glory of God in the face of Christ" (2 Corinthians 4:6).

Illumination begins as the Spirit convicts the unbeliever's heart "of guilt in regard to sin and righteousness and judgment" (John 16:8). Upon repentance and God-given faith, the Spirit regenerates the sinner (Titus 3:5), constituting him a "new creation" (2 Corinthians 5:17) and witnessing that he or she is a child of God (Romans 8:15,16). Powerful, personal assurance of faith is one of the early aspects of illumination (Galatians 4:6), reassuring the fledgling follower of Christ of the supernatural work that has occurred in his heart. John notes in his first epistle, "We know that we live in him and he in us, because he has given us of his Spirit" (4:13).

Illumination continues also in the intellectual and spiritual growth of the Christian believer. Several startling statements in John's epistle emphatically make that point: "You have an anointing from the Holy One, and all of you know the truth" (1 John 2:20). "The anointing you received from him remains in you, and you do not need anyone to teach you. . . . His anointing teaches you about all things" (2:27).

These passages cannot mean the Christian needs neither teachers nor instruction. The abundance of teaching in the New Testament would be invalidated—including John's own epistle. They do mean, however, that the Holy Spirit is a vital force within the Christian always striving against error and always tending toward truth. Confronted with sinful ideas or practices, the Holy Spirit will convict the heart. When the believer is challenged by truth, the Spirit will provide an inner affirmation of it.

The believer's acquisition of spiritual knowledge is always personal. Christianity is not a system of ideas so much as it is a relationship with God by His Spirit. Observe the progress in Paul's life: "God, who set me apart . . . was pleased to reveal his Son in me so that I might preach him among the Gentiles" (Galatians 1:15,16). Paul could not preach the reality of faith until he had first *experienced* the personal presence of Christ. The illumination of the Holy Spirit is intended first to show believers how to live with Christ and second to assist them in telling others how to live.

Illumination and the Teaching Gift

While every Christian shares in the Holy Spirit's illuminating work, it would appear that the Spirit particularly gifts some to teach. The New Testament clearly teaches that there is a class of spiritual gifts designed to equip the saints for service in the body of Christ (cf. Romans 12:6–8; 1 Corinthians 12:28–30; Ephesians 4:7–13; 1 Peter 4:10,11), and prominent among these is the gift of teaching. In Romans 12:7, Paul writes, "If it [a person's gift] is teaching, let him teach."

Teachers were ranked high in the order of the Early Church, as seen in 1 Corinthians 12:28: "In the church God has appointed first of all apostles, second prophets, third teachers." In Ephesians 4:11 the pastoral and teaching functions are drawn together in what appears to be one office, the pastor-teacher, leading one to conclude that an important and necessary function of the pastoral office is teaching. In 1 Timothy 5:17, Paul notes that elders, presumably local pastors, who rule well are to be counted "worthy of double honor, especially those whose work is preaching and teaching." Once again, the teaching function is vitally joined to the pastoral.

One of the qualifications for an overseer—probably a pastor with a distinct ruling or leadership function in the local church or churches—is that he be "able to teach" (1 Timothy 3:2). In Titus, the elder and the overseer seem to be the same person, and it is noted that "he must hold firmly to the trustworthy message as it has been taught, so that he can encourage others by sound doctrine and refute those who oppose it" (1:9).

Paul's instructions to Timothy stress the importance of the teaching office. He tells Timothy to "teach these things . . . set an example for the believers in speech, in life, in love, in faith and in purity. Until I come, devote yourself to the public reading of Scripture, to preaching, and to teaching. *Do not neglect your gift*" (1 Timothy 4:11–14, emphasis added).

The word *gift* is the Greek word *charisma*, which usually means a spiritual gift. The implication is that the Holy Spirit had uniquely gifted Timothy to carry out the above-mentioned ministries pertaining to the pastoral teaching of a local Christian church. The Holy Spirit's illumination was essential to Timothy's personal experience of faith, his intellectual grasp of faith, and his communication of faith to his parishioners.

Paul instructed Timothy not only to be a teacher of the truths of the gospel, but also to pass along what he had learned from the aging apostle to "reliable men who will also be qualified to teach others" (2 Timothy 2:2). As Timothy moved to carry out his instructions the Holy Spirit would select, gift, and illuminate specific persons in the local church to carry on the vital task of teaching the truths of the faith.

The dependence of the early teachers on the illumination and power of the Holy Spirit may be seen in a little vignette of church life in Acts 13:1–3. After the Word of the Lord had spread to Antioch, resulting in a great revival and an ingathering of believers, the church sent Barnabas to assume pastoral responsibility. Barnabas, in turn, went to Tarsus to solicit Paul's help and together they taught the church at Antioch for a whole year (11:19–26). It was while the prophets and *teachers,* now including also Simeon, Lucius, and Manaen, "were worshiping the Lord and fasting," that the Holy Spirit directed that Paul and Barnabas be sent out for their first missionary journey (13:2,3).

Once again, the importance of the teaching function in the local church is readily apparent as is the teachers' dynamic personal experience of faith and reliance upon the leadership and empowering of the Holy Spirit. Nor should it be concluded that study and thought were not necessary to such a teaching ministry. Little is known about the education of the other teachers at Antioch, but clearly Paul was one of the best educated men in the Early Church, trained, as noted earlier, at the feet of the greatest rabbi of his time.

The Early Church placed a great deal of emphasis on teaching and on the appointment and training of those who would carry on the ever-enlarging task of training a growing church. It appears that the teaching office was not concentrated in the hands of a few key pastors—who would have been inadequate for the task—but was in fact broadly diffused throughout the Church, as the Holy Spirit gave the teaching gift and illuminated those so gifted. Surely the need for the teaching gift and

the Spirit's illumination are no less critical today than in the
first century. In fact, given the size of the Church worldwide,
the need would appear more critical.

It might also be suggested that the Spirit gifts persons to
teach at many different levels. The apostles were the authoritative teachers of the Early Church but many others were
gifted and trained at subordinate levels. It is surely reasonable,
and scriptural, to understand that the Holy Spirit will gift men
and women in the church to teach at every stage of instruction
from the nursery to elementary, high school, and college students, to young and senior adults. Each age has its own unique
requirements and its own needs for technical knowledge and
expertise. A teacher may well grow from one class to another.
But the experience of the Spirit's gifting and illumination will
be common to all true Christian teachers who take their calling
seriously.

Illumination and the Spontaneous Gifts

As seen above, the teaching gift is resident in the believer
and may be exercised any time the teacher chooses. Another
and perhaps better known group of spiritual gifts is found in
1 Corinthians 12:8–10. These may be called spontaneous gifts
since not only are they given by the Spirit (12:7) but they can
be manifested only at the Spirit's direction. The believer cannot
use them whenever he chooses.

Among these spontaneous gifts, which the Spirit will customarily channel through particular persons, are several related to the teaching function and hence to the illuminating
work of the Holy Spirit. Prophecy is the most notable example.
"Everyone who prophesies speaks to men for their strength-
ening, encouragement and comfort," Paul wrote (1 Corinthians
14:3). The church is enriched in understanding and in spirit by
a true prophecy and it is impossible to conclude that the illuminating work of the Spirit is not at work in the one who
delivers the prophecy. Interpreted tongues seem to have the
same value (14:5), and it is probable that something of the

teaching/illuminating ministry of the Spirit is in the "message of wisdom" and the "message of knowledge" (12:8).

Paul found it necessary to correct some deficiencies in the practice of these gifts by the Corinthians. They tended to give the utterances absolute authority. Whatever was spoken was assumed to be directly from God. Paul laid down some careful guidelines to ensure that spontaneous messages would be held accountable to the truths of the Christian faith. In 1 Corinthians 14:29, he limits prophetic messages (as he does tongues) to two or three. Once spoken, those messages were to be carefully weighed to ensure that they were indeed quickened by the Spirit and in keeping with the revealed truths of the Christian faith.

Paul also exhorted the Thessalonians, "Do not put out the Spirit's fire; do not treat prophecies with contempt." But he added the ever-needed caution, "Test everything. *Hold on to the good"* (1 Thessalonians 5:19–21, emphasis added). The believers at Thessalonica would have thrown out the baby with the bathwater.

John also taught such a testing of the prophets: "Dear friends, do not believe every spirit, but test the spirits to see whether they are from God, because many false prophets have gone out into the world" (1 John 4:1). John's test was simple: "This is how you can recognize the Spirit of God: Every spirit that acknowledges that Jesus Christ has come in the flesh is from God, but every spirit that does not acknowledge Jesus is not from God" (4:2,3). So every utterance was brought to the touchstone of the gospel and if it did not match up, it was rejected.

In fact, submission to the revelation of the Scriptures was held to be the mark of a truly spiritual person. "If anybody thinks he is a prophet or spiritually gifted, let him acknowledge that what I am writing to you is the Lord's command" (1 Corinthians 14:37). Charisma, power, attractiveness, and persuasiveness all counted for nothing if the gospel was not correctly taught in the message. The written Word was the acid test for every utterance.

Spiritual Discipline

Illumination retains a necessary dependence on the Holy Spirit throughout the life of the believer. Coming initially as a miraculous, seemingly effortless impartation of the Spirit in personal salvation, illumination thereafter is related to the believer's spiritual discipline.

The Christian who is careless in prayer, the reading of the Scriptures, and attendance at worship services will find a diminishing intensity of personal understanding and growth in spiritual matters. Such lackluster faith was a problem in biblical times just as it is today. Paul wrote to the schismatic Corinthians, "Brothers, I could not address you as spiritual but as worldly—mere infants in Christ. I gave you milk, not solid food, for you were not yet ready for it" (1 Corinthians 3:1,2).

The writer to the Hebrews complained that his charges were "slow to learn. In fact, though by this time you ought to be teachers, you need someone to teach you the elementary truths of God's word all over again. You need milk, not solid food" (Hebrews 5:11,12). Then he added, "Solid food is for the mature, who by constant use have trained themselves to distinguish good from evil" (v. 14). Clearly these Christians had not cultivated the spiritual discipline that allowed the Holy Spirit to properly illuminate their minds and hearts for personal growth and teaching ministry.

By contrast, however, the convert who covets a truly Spirit-filled life of fellowship, study, and service may expect to grow continuously in understanding for his own life and for ministry to others. Regular prayer from a contrite heart ready to accept the correction of God's Word will open one to a rich personal relationship with the Holy Spirit who is the source of all true spiritual illumination. The Bible will loom large in daily life as the believer reads it devotionally, studies it for personal growth and ministry, memorizes from it, meditates on it, discusses it, and listens to sermons and lessons based on it. Good books on spiritual devotion, doctrine, and biblical interpretation will help.

A conscientious believer confronted with new ideas will ask, "Does the Bible really say that?" and "Is what seems to be taught in this one passage borne out elsewhere in the Bible?" The Spirit's work of illumination will proceed very rapidly under such conditions, and a new Christian will move expeditiously toward mature faith and ministry.

It should be remembered, however, that the Christian life is still a growth process. As the Spirit and the Word work hand in hand in the life of the believer, his understanding will widen and deepen over the years. Some early fervently held beliefs will be found not truly in accord with Scripture and will need to be modified or abandoned. Other fresh and powerful new truths will be discovered. Since we are human and begin with such limited knowledge, it should not be surprising that we will make many midcourse corrections of life and thought.

An inspiring biblical formula for the life open to the Spirit's illumination might be the command of Paul in Colossians 3:16: "Let the word of Christ dwell in you richly as you teach and admonish one another with all wisdom, and as you sing psalms, hymns and spiritual songs with gratitude in your hearts to God."

Cautions

Every biblical truth can be pushed to an unbiblical extreme. This is debilitating for the individual Christian and the church as a whole. The doctrine of illumination is certainly one capable of such abuse and should be safeguarded by certain common-sense qualifications found in the Scriptures.

Spiritual illumination requires total honesty and sincerity before God and His Word. Peter took note of the fact that, in his day, "ignorant and unstable people" were distorting Paul's writings, which were often hard to understand, "to their own destruction" (2 Peter 3:16). There is always the temptation to use the Bible for selfish reasons, selecting and perhaps twisting certain passages to support popular ideas and life-styles while neglecting other passages that show the fallacy of the desired interpretation. The Spirit of truth will struggle continuously against such mishandling of God's Word, but He can be rejected, grieved, and finally dismissed from the human heart.

Illumination does not grant infallibility to the Christian's preaching or teaching. Infallibility, or inerrancy, is a God-breathed quality that inheres only in the Scriptures, not in the believer. Thus a Christian preacher's or teacher's message is infallible only to the extent that he or she has correctly expressed the biblical teaching in its larger context. Even then, the message is without error only because it is the Word of God, not because the believer, Spirit-filled and illuminated though he may be, has spoken it.

Illumination, as shown above, does not grant infallibility to any spiritual utterance. All prophecies, messages in tongues, or messages of wisdom and knowledge must be held accountable to the written Word. In this way the church may be assured of the needed dynamism of the Spirit's presence and at the same time be protected against the excesses of emotion and carnality.

Illumination is not revelation. It does not convey factual information to the believer as he pores over or reflects upon the Word. One should not expect the Spirit to reveal the date of the Book of Daniel or the interpretation of Daniel's unusual visions apart from careful study. The Spirit will not unlock the meaning of Hebrew or Greek for those who have never learned those languages. Only careful comparison of Scripture passage with Scripture passage will yield the significance of the "abomination of desolation" (Matthew 24:15, KJV) or the vexing symbolism of the Book of Revelation. Rather, the Holy Spirit works as a guide through the natural faculties of human beings as they are vigorously utilized and reverently yielded to Him, gently affirming truth and convicting of error.

Every Christian at some point has probably wished he could have walked with Jesus. Although that is impossible, every generation of Christians has the next best thing. Jesus had been the disciples' Counselor during His ministry with them. As the time to depart approached, He told them, "I will ask the Father, and he will give you another Counselor to be with you forever—the Spirit of truth." Then Jesus added that the Counselor would be "in" the disciples (John 14:16,17). Rather than being totally dependent on Jesus' physical presence, the time would come when the disciples would have His spiritual presence and message internalized in each of them—everywhere and at all times.

Every Christian throughout the ages has had the privilege of the indwelling presence of the Spirit of truth to lead him to the fullest experience and understanding of faith. To quote again the Beloved Disciple, "You have an anointing from the Holy One, and all of you know the truth" (1 John 2:20).

6

The Holy Spirit and the Student: Coming To Know Christ

ZENAS J. BICKET

The student, or learner, is the one for whom the entire Christian education program is designed and carried out. Indeed, the learner is the one for whom God's plan of salvation and spiritual growth has been set in motion. The teacher, the pastor, the evangelist, and every leadership office of the Church are important, but each leader is first a student who must go through the learning and growth process.

God did not send His Son just for the benefit of teachers and pastors. He gave pastors, teachers, apostles, evangelists, and every other ministry gift for the benefit of ordinary people: the world (the unsaved) and the Church (believers). "God so loved the world, that he gave his only begotten Son" (John 3:16, KJV). "He . . . gave . . . apostles, . . . prophets, . . . evangelists, . . . pastors and teachers" (Ephesians 4:11). Of course, God gives generously *to* His pastors, teachers, and so on; as individuals they are part of the Church, His body. But whatever leadership gifts God bestows on them are for the edification of others.

The Holy Spirit was promised by Jesus as He was about to return to the Father. "I will send Him to you. . . . When He . . . has come, He will guide you into all truth; . . . He will tell you

Zenas J. Bicket, Ph.D. in literature, is dean of curriculum and instructional design at Berean College of the Assemblies of God, Springfield, Missouri.

things to come" (John 16:7,13, NKJV). The promised Comforter
has been sent for 20th-century believers just as much as for
first-century disciples. What a blessed Helper and Friend!

Fear of the Holy Ghost

Some children and adults have an unwholesome fear of the
Holy Ghost. Children might be excused for such fear because
of their limited understanding. But too many adults—Christian adults—are not quite sure that this Comforter is really
their personal Friend. The mystery of the supernatural is beyond their finite comprehension, and they have not yet learned
simple trust in a benevolent God. They may even imagine a
supernatural evil supplanting the good.

The translators of the King James Version did not intend
that readers should think of the Holy Spirit as a disembodied
ghost. In the 16th century, the words *ghost* and *spirit* meant
the same thing. Children and some adults think of ghosts as
spirits of dead people that appear to living persons as pale,
shadowy apparitions. That misconception may hinder their
complete submission to the working of the Holy Spirit.

The Holy Spirit is a special personal Friend. Solomon's description of "a friend who sticks closer than a brother" (Proverbs 18:24) could certainly be applied to the Holy Spirit. Such
a Friend would not allow anyone who is sincerely and scrip-
turally seeking the Lord to be misled by a counterfeit spirit.

The Age of Accountability

When can a child understand that the Holy Spirit is a special
Friend? More important, when can a child understand the basics
of the plan of salvation, and at what age is he held accountable
for accepting or rejecting God's grace and the salvation provided by Christ's death on the cross?

The *age of accountability* has been defined by some as the
age of 12. There is, however, no New Testament basis for choosing this age, nor is the phrase found anywhere in the Scrip-

tures. The idea probably originates from the practice of ushering the Jewish male into the adult community and legal responsibilities at the age of 12. It can be assumed that every child, no matter how slow the development of his moral consciousness, is fully aware and understands his obligations by the age of 12.

But most children come to an awareness of right and wrong, and of the importance of choosing the right over the wrong, long before reaching the age of 12. Only God knows the actual age of accountability for each individual. Parents and teachers must constantly consider that each child may at any time be coming to that awareness that makes him accountable. There are no "free years" when a parent or a teacher can relax, thinking that nurturing and spiritual instruction begin with some future age of accountability. Many a child has unfortunately been lost from the Kingdom because adults have underestimated the comprehension and spiritual development of the young one.

One modern school of psychology sees man as an advanced animal. Like animals, which act out of instinct and natural inclination, man does only what his natural inclinations lead him to do. Therefore, he cannot be held responsible for wrongdoing or sin, for his actions supposedly are the result of forces beyond his control. Man is viewed as no more than an animal without a soul or a moral conscience.

The absurdity of this position is easily demonstrated. If everyone really believed that man will never be required to give account for his choices and actions, anarchy would result. When everyone looks out only for himself, the world becomes cruel and frightening. Yet that is the direction in which our world seems to be moving.

The age of divine accountability is the age at which each student can comprehend right and wrong and understand the way of salvation.

The Work of the Holy Spirit in Salvation

Every true Christian knows that without the drawing of the

Holy Spirit he would never have turned to God for salvation through Jesus Christ. Yet even before man is aware of the Spirit's drawing, the Spirit is actively *restraining* the evil forces that seek to destroy each soul. Satan delights in destroying people before they can make their decision to accept Christ as Savior. But the Holy Spirit prevents this from happening. "When the enemy comes in like a flood, the Spirit of the Lord will lift up a standard against him" (Isaiah 59:19, NKJV). The Spirit certainly raises up a standard in behalf of every tested Christian, but we must never forget that a loving God is faithfully restraining the devil to give each soul a chance to know divine mercy and grace.

The Holy Spirit also actively *convicts* the unbeliever of sin. " 'When He has come, He will convict the world of sin, and of righteousness, and of judgment: of sin, because they do not believe in Me; of righteousness, because I go to My Father . . . ; of judgment, because the ruler of this world is judged' " (John 16:8–11, NKJV). Mankind's sin and approaching judgment are made plain by the Holy Spirit.

The word translated "convict" *(elegcho)* is rendered in other versions as "reprove" or "convince." The original word, used 17 times in the New Testament, refers to the process whereby a person is caused to reach certain conclusions *in his mind.* This meaning is somewhat removed from the common idea that conviction is an emotion, a spiritual depression and sorrow for sin. In reality, the emotion that is experienced is the result of conviction (the convinced state of mind). The great contrast between the convinced knowledge of God's holiness and the awareness of personal unrighteousness causes in the sinner the emotion commonly called conviction.

The Holy Spirit convicts or convinces of three things as He begins to lead the sinner to an experiential faith in the redemptive work of Jesus Christ. He convinces of *sin* (v. 9). He enlightens the sinner about his sinful condition (not just his individual sins). The Spirit reveals to the unsaved the all-encompassing sin of rejecting Christ.

The Holy Spirit convicts or convinces the sinner about *righteousness* (v. 10). He enlightens the sinner concerning the great distance between God's righteousness and man's. Like the disobedient Israelites, "We are all like an unclean thing, and all our righteousnesses are like filthy rags" (Isaiah 64:6, NKJV). Because Jesus has gone to the Father, He sits at the right hand pleading His righteousness as a substitute for our filthy rags. The Spirit convinces of righteousness.

The Holy Spirit convicts or convinces the sinner of *judgment* (John 16:11). He reminds him that sin and Satan have already been judged and conquered. Although sin must be judged and punished, God's attitude toward the sinner has completely changed because Christ died to remove the penalty that should fall on the sinner. The sinner need do nothing to appease God. He must only be convinced of the realities of sin, righteousness, and judgment and then completely rely on God's saving grace.

EXAMPLES OF CONVICTION

When Peter finished his sermon to the multitude at Jerusalem on the Day of Pentecost, "They were cut to the heart and said to Peter and the other apostles, 'Brothers, what shall we do?' " (Acts 2:37). The Spirit, as Peter was speaking to them, convinced them that Peter's words were true. The people not only were moved, but also realized they needed to do something. Both their minds and hearts were touched.

A chaplain walked up and down the aisle outside the death-row cells at a state penitentiary. Wherever possible, he stopped to share a witness for Christ. But in cell after cell, the response was the same, "The judge was unfair," "I didn't commit any crime," or "The real criminal got off scot-free." Toward the end of the block was an inmate who sat on his cot with his head in his hands. In response to the chaplain's attempt to minister, a sob broke from the man's lips. "I've blown it; no one is to blame but myself. I feel rotten, miserable." The convict was the first convert in the chaplain's prison ministry.

"The Lord is near to those who have a broken heart, and

saves such as have a contrite spirit" (Psalm 34:18, NKJV). Furthermore, God never despises or ignores a broken spirit and a contrite heart (Psalm 51:17) whether He finds it in a sinner or a believer. But only the Holy Spirit can effect the change from a naturally hard, rebellious heart to a tender, repentant heart.

The prophet Isaiah had a transforming experience as a young man. Whether he had any similar confrontations with the majesty and holiness of God before the one recorded in Isaiah 6, we do not know. Following the vision, he cried out, "Woe is me, for I am undone" (6:5, NKJV). He repented for what he was, not for what he had done. "I am a man of unclean lips" (v. 5). He could have said, "Forgive me for telling this lie, or for dishonoring Your name with my lips." Even though Isaiah spoke many truthful and God-honoring words, the Spirit had revealed to him that he was a man of unclean lips. His greatest righteousness was filthy alongside God's righteousness. The transformation was complete when Isaiah responded, "Here am I. Send me!" (v. 8).

Examples of the Spirit's conviction are many in Acts, the book of the outpouring of the Spirit. At his Damascus Road experience, the apostle Paul, "trembling and astonished, said, 'Lord, what do You want me to do?' " (9:6, NKJV). The Philippian jailer, so emotionally distraught that he was about to commit suicide, "fell trembling before Paul and Silas . . . and asked, 'Sirs, what must I do to be saved?' " (16:29,30). In response to Paul's anointed defense of the gospel, "Felix was afraid, and answered, 'Go away for now; when I have a convenient time I will call for you' " (24:25, NKJV). The convicting power of the Holy Spirit was evident as King Agrippa told Paul, " 'You almost persuade me to become a Christian' " (26:28, NKJV). The Holy Spirit convicts or convinces, but it still rests with man to act on that conviction. Felix and Agrippa did not.

THE GREAT AWAKENING

The Great Awakening was a religious revival of unusual

proportions that swept the American colonies between 1740 and 1745. Among the leaders in the awakening were Jonathan Edwards, George Whitefield, and David Brainard. Edwards' sermon, "Sinners in the Hands of an Angry God," has come to characterize the revival for many people today. The move of the Spirit in conviction and regeneration, however, are more representative characteristics of the revival.

In his *Memoirs,* a journal of his spiritual growth and ministry among the American Indians, David Brainard recounts some of the results of the Spirit's powerful conviction: "Old men were also in distress for their souls; so that they could not refrain from weeping and crying aloud; and their bitter groans were the most convincing as well as affecting evidence of the reality and depth of their inward anguish" (journal entry for August 16, 1745).

After preaching to the Indians on another occasion,

> The power of God seemed to descend upon the assembly *"like a mighty rushing wind,"* and with an astonishing energy bore down all before it. I stood amazed at the influence, which seized the audience almost universally . . . . Almost all persons of all ages were bowed down with concern together. . . . Old men and women, who had been drunken wretches for many years, and some little children, not more than six or seven years of age, appeared in distress for their souls (journal entry for August 8, 1745).

But such emotional responses to the move of the Spirit were not well received by the established institutions of the day. Yale and Harvard universities took a stand against the revival and against the emotional outbursts which they felt to be inappropriate. Yet the impact of the revival, in the form of changed lives, was confirmation enough that the move of the Spirit was genuine.

OPPOSITION VOICES TODAY

Many persons today are opposed to what evangelical Chris-

tians describe as conviction. Humanistic psychology empha-
sizes man's right to be free from all feelings of guilt and in-
feriority. The message preached in the secular classroom and
written in popular psychology paperbacks is "I'm O.K., and you
are too."

In the face of these opposition voices, the church speaks less
and less about the conviction of the Holy Spirit and about the
emotional responses that sometimes result from that inner conviction. But conviction is simply "being made conscious of guilt."
When man is not living in right relationship with God, conviction is a supernatural move of the Spirit on his life, not a
self-induced psychological state to be denied or explained away.

The Great Awakening is a title given to a revival over two
centuries ago. God does not move—nor can we require that He
do so—in the same way in every revival or spiritual renewal.
It is interesting to note, however, that many of the manifestations of the Spirit's work in salvation seen in biblical and
other historical accounts have had their counterpart in the
Pentecostal revival of the 20th century. The bringing of men
and women to a salvation experience with Jesus Christ, through
the convicting work of the Holy Spirit, is just one example of
the timelessness of the New Testament message.

But whether it happened in the 1740s or happens again in
the 1990s, every person, every Sunday school student, must
experience his own "great awakening"—an awakening to his
lost condition without Christ; an awakening to the sinful, fallen
nature that defeats every human attempt at righteousness; an
awakening to the reality of a judgment awaiting every person
who rejects the sacrificial death of Christ as the means of his
salvation. Out of this awakening comes the resurrection awakening as the sinner becomes a new creation in Christ.

WHAT PRODUCES CONVICTION?

Conviction is produced by an interaction of three things: the

Word, the Holy Spirit, and the conscience of man. After Peter preached his sermon on the Day of Pentecost, quoting generously from the books of Joel and the Psalms, the Spirit drove the inspired Word home to the hearts of the crowd (Acts 2). The Children of Israel wept when the Word was read publicly by Ezra (Nehemiah 8:9). In response to Jesus' invitation for a sinless person to cast the first stone at the woman taken in the act of adultery, the accusers went out one by one "being convicted by their own conscience" (John 8:9, KJV).

The role of the Holy Spirit and of the Word in the working of conviction is plain, but how does the conscience enter into the experience of conviction? Is the conscience of a person reared in a heathen culture the same as that of a child reared in a Christian home? Is the conscience of a child reared in "Christian America" but not in a Christian home any different from that of his heathen counterpart across the seas? And what distinctive approaches will the Holy Spirit and the anointed teacher take in seeking to win each person to Christ?

The conscience is the inner judge of moral issues. This inborn faculty in every human being has been misunderstood and neglected. Psychologists speak of the mind, the emotions, and the will, but they seldom speak of the conscience. Yet whatever one's mind or emotions may do, the conscience sits in judgment as to whether the action was good or bad.

There is a wide range of opinion concerning the origin of the conscience. At one extreme, some have described the conscience as the voice of God speaking to the individual. But the fact that the conscience is fallible and can be defiled would refute that explanation. At the opposite extreme, others contend that the conscience is an acquired attitude of mind, a system of values formed by early training. The deficiency in this explanation is that even heathen or uncivilized people who are taught no moral values have a sense of right and wrong.

An individual conscience is described in various Scripture passages as good (Acts 23:1), pure (1 Timothy 3:9, NKJV), evil (Hebrews 10:22, NKJV), weak and defiled (1 Corinthians 8:7), and seared (1 Timothy 4:2). The conscience can act as a witness (Romans 2:15), an accuser that convicts (John 8:9, KJV), a protector against spiritual shipwreck (1 Timothy 1:19), and a source of joy (2 Corinthians 1:12, KJV). It sometimes needs cleansing (Hebrews 9:14). It is not infallible (Proverbs 16:25). The values held by different individuals, as determined by their consciences, are different (1 Corinthians 8:7–13). And one person's conscience must sometimes be subject to the conscience of another person (1 Corinthians 10:28,29).

The Bible depicts the conscience as an inherent part of human nature that is subject to abuse and defilement. In spite of the possibility of abuse and misuse, it serves as a monitor of human actions. The exciting thing about the Spirit-filled life is that the Holy Spirit can work in and through the conscience to guide the believer's thoughts and conduct.

So we conclude that the child born in a heathen home, the one born in a nonreligious home in "Christian America," and the child born in a Christian home all originally were given the same kind of conscience by their Creator. Yet by the time the two American children attend Sunday school, the values held by the conscience of each will be different. However, as the teacher faithfully teaches the Word, the Holy Spirit can retrain and restore the original conscience and lead the individual to a salvation experience.

FROM CONVICTION TO SALVATION

A teacher should never seek to bypass the stage of conviction in leading a student to faith in Jesus Christ. Conviction makes the salvation experience more meaningful and lasting. If the believer is later tempted to question the reality of his salvation, remembering the indelible impression of sin's burden (made so real by the Holy Spirit) will make the salvation experience stick.

How does a teacher recognize that a student is experiencing the conviction of the Holy Spirit? The signs are not the same in all individuals, for each person responds differently to the work of the Spirit. However, the teacher should be alert to the following characteristics:

1. A new attentiveness and interest in spiritual concerns may signal an awakening of the heart. When the sinner "has ears to hear," the way of salvation will be shared by the Spirit.

2. A new sensitivity and tenderness (a contrite heart) is also an indication that the Spirit is at work in the life of the student.

3. Some may even manifest the signs of conviction that were so prevalent during the Great Awakening: fear of eternal damnation, distress, and feelings of helplessness and unworthiness. Since the true conviction of the Holy Spirit is for the purpose of bringing the sinner to salvation, these feelings should not persist indefinitely. A supernatural peace and victory come with the decision to accept Jesus Christ.

4. Some sinners respond to the conviction of the Holy Spirit with belligerence and rebellion. This sign of conviction is sometimes misinterpreted or overlooked. The sinner who has been convinced of his sinfulness may not at first accept the verdict very kindly. The teacher may need to show great patience with a student who is experiencing this type of conviction.

The work of the Holy Spirit in man's salvation does not end with conviction. We have seen how the Holy Spirit restrains Satan from destroying the soul of the sinner until he has a chance to accept Christ as his personal Savior. The Spirit's work of conviction has been a major emphasis of this chapter. But the Holy Spirit also works to regenerate the sinner who is dead in trespasses and sin. *Regeneration* is not the gaining of additional knowledge, moral or ethical improvement, being baptized in water, or joining a church. It is not something added to what we are. It is a complete change—an exchange of the old life for a new one.

Regeneration is also called the new birth, or being born again. When a repenting sinner accepts Christ as Savior, the Holy Spirit gives him a new nature. Jesus explained the role of the

Spirit in salvation to Nicodemus in John 3: "Unless a man is born of water and *the Spirit,* he cannot enter the kingdom of God" (v. 5, emphasis added). Regeneration is an act of divine creation; the Holy Spirit is the agent. We are truly born of the Spirit.

The Holy Spirit also cooperates with Christ in achieving our *justification.* The word *justify* is a judicial term meaning to acquit, to declare righteous. At the moment of salvation, the guilty sinner stands before God, the righteous Judge; but instead of a sentence of condemnation, he receives a sentence of acquittal. Justification is God's declaration that we are righteous, in spite of the sin and disobedience that filled our lives before the supernatural miracle of God's grace.

All sin is disobedience against God and must be judged. But when sinful man comes to the Great Judge and asks forgiveness for his disobedience, the Judge says, "I declare you righteous." The past is forgiven and forgotten and man's relationship to God is restored to what it was intended to be before the Fall. All guilt, condemnation, and separation are removed by the act of justification. "Who will bring any charge against those whom God has chosen? It is God who justifies" (Romans 8:33).

Justification is more than pardon. A pardoned criminal is not regarded as being righteous. He is only pardoned from the penalty of his crime. But the Christian is declared righteous. Justification goes beyond forgiveness. Justification declares one to be righteous and then demonstrates toward the justified person an attitude that says, "You are just as righteous as if you had never sinned." The Holy Spirit who convicts the sinner of his need for a Savior brings together the repentant sinner and the One who died for his sins.

The Spirit and the Student—Coming To Know Christ

The Holy Spirit testifies to every Sunday school student about the person and work of Jesus Christ. Through the testimony of believers—teachers, pastors, evangelists, missionaries—He constantly bears witness to sinful man that Christ died for his sins. To be a link in the many-faceted chain that turns a hell-bound student toward a heaven-bound eternity is one of the greatest privileges God gives His children. With the help of the Spirit your ministry for the Kingdom will be blessed and fruitful!

7

The Holy Spirit and the Student: Victorious Christian Living

ZENAS J. BICKET

A woman living in a small eastern city experienced some strange happenings in her home. No matter where she set her radio dial, only one station came in—the 50,000-watt station broadcasting from a tower located just blocks from her home. But then things got worse. In the middle of the night, without any radio set turned on, music would start playing. A metal-frame bed and the entire electrical wiring system of her home were serving as antennas to pick up and broadcast the programming. Invisible radio waves were so powerful they intruded even when they were not wanted.

The time is the middle of the week. One of the students to whom you regularly minister each Sunday sits alone in his room. He is lonely as he faces a burden by himself, a burden he is afraid to share with anyone else. You ministered to him just a few days ago but are unaware of his struggle. There are powerful "waves" in his room that cannot be picked up by a radio receiver, but these waves will not violently intrude. The powerful Presence in the room is the omnipresent Holy Spirit, the Comforter and Helper you tried to introduce to your student just days before.

Mulling over the circumstances of the conflict that shattered his day, the student remembers your straight-forward declaration that the Holy Spirit will help any believer who calls on Him. His thoughts turn to God, with the prayer that what you said on Sunday is really true on Tuesday.

As promised, a Power begins to work in the room and in his heart. A temper that was out of control begins to learn gentleness and kindness. A sluggish, apathetic attitude is transformed into a purposeful determination to make his life count for God. A timid and cowardly spirit grows bold through the encouragement of the Holy Spirit.

Sometimes your divine commission to share the Word with your world seems unfulfilled. But when you team up with the Spirit in the work of witnessing and teaching, your faithful labor has results even when you are caught up in your daily routine. The powerful waves of the Spirit are always there. It is a wonderful privilege to introduce your students to the greatest Friend and Helper.

The Continuing Work of the Holy Spirit

The Holy Spirit does not leave after He convicts, convinces, and finally leads the sinner to accept Jesus Christ as Savior. When He has made a new creature in place of the old man, His work has only begun. Were the Spirit to leave, the new Christian would soon slip back into his former sins. David realized the importance of the continuing presence of the Spirit in his life. "Do not take Your Holy Spirit from me," he prayed (Psalm 51:11, NKJV). He knew that at the time of his failure and sin, he needed the cleansing and restoring presence of God's Spirit more than ever.

How did you conclude your lesson last Sunday? With a funny story? With an evangelistic appeal? With a frustrated "There's the bell; we have to quit"?

There is an appropriate ending for every lesson you and the Holy Spirit teach. The variety of effective conclusions is limitless, but they should all communicate this: The lessons learned in the classroom on Sunday must be put into practice during the week, and the Holy Spirit will be with the student to help translate theory into practice.

On some occasions, the Spirit may lead you to conclude the class session with an appeal to make a commitment right on the spot: a commitment to let Christ come into the student's life or to obediently yield to the work that the Holy Spirit wants to do in his life.

SANCTIFICATION AND HOLINESS

The most important thing the Spirit wants to do in your students is to develop a sanctified or holy life. Believers should not remain what they were immediately after conversion. We are to become more and more like Christ. This process of becoming more like Him is called progressive sanctification; it is distinct from instantaneous (positional) sanctification, which takes place at the moment of salvation.

As we daily become more like Jesus, four things happen in our lives. First, we more completely present our lives to God. "I beseech you therefore, brethren, by the mercies of God, that you present your bodies a living sacrifice, holy, acceptable to God, which is your reasonable service" (Romans 12:1, NKJV).

Second, we grow from spiritual infancy toward spiritual maturity (1 Corinthians 3:1; 2 Peter 3:18). Third, we are continually cleansed and purified from all filthiness of the flesh and the spirit (2 Corinthians 7:1). Finally, we are transformed, day by day, into a more Christlike person. The Holy Spirit is the primary Agent in bringing about these changes in our lives.

Sanctification is a process that continues throughout a believer's lifetime. It is positive rather than negative. A person is not considered holy because of the things he does not do. Holiness is not judged by the vices from which a Christian abstains. Instead, it is the positive conformation to the image of Christ.

Some teach an experience of sanctification which they call a second definite work of grace. But there is nothing in the Scriptures to suggest that a Christian, in this life, will ever achieve a state where he will never sin again. "If we say that we have no sin, we deceive ourselves, and the truth is not in us" (1 John 1:8, NKJV). If such a sanctification were possible, our struggles would be much easier. But the flesh never becomes spiritual. The most saintly human being must contend with the flesh until complete and final sanctification at the coming of Jesus Christ or deliverance from the body through death. We are sanctified by the Holy Spirit, who repeatedly gives us victory over the flesh (Romans 15:16).

THE BAPTISM IN THE HOLY SPIRIT

The Holy Spirit works in the lives of all believers after conversion to make them more like Jesus—to sanctify and make them holy. But there is an experience that holds the potential for accelerating the process of making us more Christlike, both in character and service. It is described in Acts 2 and is the distinctive belief of all Christians who call themselves Pentecostals.

The Book of Acts can be embarrassing reading, not because of inappropriate content, but because many Christian churches today are not at all like the descriptions we read in Acts. The New Testament church expanded with a rapidity that puts 20th-century evangelism to shame, even with its modern techniques of communication and outreach. The only hope of having a New Testament church today is a repeat of the Pentecostal experience in many, many lives, and especially in the life of every Sunday school student.

Right now, in many denominations (both Pentecostal and non-Pentecostal), believers are asking God for the infilling of the Holy Spirit. And they are not being disappointed. Either individually in private prayer, or in the company of Spirit-filled believers, they are being baptized in the Holy Spirit and speaking in other tongues as did the disciples on the Day of Pentecost.

The disciples were gathered together in the Upper Room waiting for the promise as Jesus had commanded them. Then it happened! The sound of wind, the cloven tongues of fire, the speaking in tongues! Some claim the promise was completely fulfilled at this event. But Peter said it was just a beginning:

"The promise is for you and your children and for all who are far off—for all whom the Lord our God will call" (Acts 2:39). The last decade of the 20th century is as far off in time as the world has ever been. The promise is for us too!

How is the experience received? In much the same way salvation is received. A right attitude is essential. The 120 on whom the Spirit was first outpoured knew unity and prayed in one accord. Obedience to God is necessary because God gives the Holy Spirit "to those who obey him" (Acts 5:32). Just as faith is required in salvation, so we must have faith to receive this gift for anointed service and holy living.

How does the student know he has received the baptism in the Holy Spirit? This question has caused much controversy and has been a major point of disagreement between Pentecostals and non-Pentecostal evangelicals.

The Pentecostal position that speaking in tongues is the initial physical evidence of the baptism in the Holy Spirit is based on the five instances of such infillings recorded in the Book of Acts (chapters 2, 8, 9, 10, 19). In three of the five accounts, the believers all spoke in Spirit-inspired languages upon receiving the Baptism. In the other two instances the speaking in other tongues is implied.

Simon the Sorcerer desired to buy the gift because of some obvious external manifestation (Acts 8). Paul experienced the manifestation at some time because he later testified that he spoke in tongues more than the believers to whom he was writing (Acts 9:17,18; 1 Corinthians 14:18). The Holy Spirit dwells in every believer, but every believer has not been baptized in the Holy Spirit.

The Spirit-Filled Life

Jonathan Edwards, the great 18th-century leader in the Great Awakening, observed that the same Holy Spirit who works on the sinner to produce conviction works on the believer to develop a delight or pleasure in such devotional exercises as singing, reading the Bible, praying, and hearing the Word preached.[1]

Nothing but a supernatural work of the Spirit could explain a sudden interest in spiritual matters from a person who previously had shown no such concern. In fact, a believer can take personal inventory of his own spiritual condition by ascertaining his level of desire for and delight in spending time in private devotions, singing, praying, and reading the Word. When people become Christians, the attitudes and actions that used to bring pleasure are no longer enjoyed; instead, the same sins cause guilt and separation from the Comforter within.

In addition to a desire to commune with Jesus, there are other evidences of a Spirit-filled life. The fruit of the Spirit— love, joy, peace, patience, gentleness, goodness, faith or faithfulness, kindness, and self-control (Galatians 5:22,23) are definite indicators of a Spirit-filled life. The characteristics of the human race as it naturally exists are the complete opposite of the fruit of the Spirit. Yet just as the tree is made perfect in the fruit, so the believer is shown to be like Christ by the fruit of the Spirit in his life.

All Christians should be encouraged to experience the baptism in the Holy Spirit and subsequently live a Spirit-filled life. The world will respond to the example and message of anointed believers.

In a primitive area of Asia, the women go outdoors each morning and look up at their neighbors' chimneys. When they see one out of which smoke is rising, they head for that home to borrow live coals with which to kindle a fire in their own homes. Sinners and believers alike are waiting to kindle the fire of their hearts from the live coals burning in the life of the Spirit-filled Christian.

POWER FOR WITNESS AND SERVICE

Students must learn to draw upon supernatural power for effective witness and service. The source of our power is not the experience of the Baptism, but Jesus Christ himself. The power is in the Giver, not in the gift. Yet it is the Holy Spirit— the wonderful gift received in fullness at the Baptism—who brings the divine power of the Godhead into our lives. So it is entirely appropriate to speak of the power of the Spirit.

One of the primary purposes for the baptism in the Holy Spirit is power to witness for Christ. The Spirit works to convict sinners and call them to salvation. But what a privilege it is to become, through the Baptism, a part of the Spirit's strategy for winning the lost. Just as the Holy Spirit was the moving force behind the effective evangelism of the Early Church, so is He today.

The Spirit-filled believer is called to witness to people who are unknowingly captives of Satan. We are called to faithfully witness; it is the Holy Spirit's task, through yielded and trusting channels, to break the chains and deliver the prisoners. The Spirit convicts the sinner of sin, righteousness, and judgment. The one who witnesses can do nothing to change the basic nature of a sinner. The Spirit makes Jesus real to people—as Savior and as Sovereign Lord.

In addition to preparing the heart and will of the sinner, the Spirit also prepares and leads the witness. The power to witness is promised after the Spirit "comes on" (clothes or endues) the believer (Acts 1:8). As the Spirit-filled believer waits on God, the Holy Spirit will guide and direct him in effective soul winning. Jesus told the disciples the Holy Spirit would give them the necessary words as needed (Mark 13:11). Education and training in evangelism methods are good, but are never substitutes for the Spirit's supernatural work. As the Spirit anoints the words spoken, divine conviction will pierce the hearts of the hearers.

Winning the lost is not a mechanical process. The soul winner must witness with divine love and compassion that can come only as the fullness of the Spirit produces these godly virtues. With the help of the Spirit, evangelism is transformed into joyful labor.

POWER IN PRAYER AND INTERCESSION

John Wesley was once asked, "With all the time you spend

in prayer, when do you do your work?" Wesley quickly responded, "Sir, prayer *is* my work."

In his own strength and intellect, the student lacks the understanding of how and for what he should pray. But beyond that, without the encouragement and inspiration of the Spirit he finds it difficult to pray, not to mention persevere in intercession for a specific burden. But "the Spirit also helps in our weaknesses. For we do not know what we should pray for as we ought, but the Spirit Himself makes intercession for us" (Romans 8:26, NKJV). No one by nature finds it easy to pray, but the Spirit creates a desire to pray and lets us know what to pray for.

It is not prayer alone that accomplishes the work of the Kingdom, but praying in the Spirit. After the baptism in the Holy Spirit, the believer's prayer life should deepen and grow more effective as he continues to walk in the fullness of the Spirit.

A good test of our spiritual maturity is the amount of time we pray for ourselves (and our small circle) as compared with the amount of time we pray for others. Satan steals our spiritual strength when we become preoccupied in our prayer times with our own concerns, especially with our weaknesses, until we have no time to engage in actual combat with Satan. Intercession involves persistent prayer for the needs of someone else. The prayer of faith in one situation will release a person instantaneously. In another case, release may come only after repeated, persevering prayer. Without the help of the Spirit, we do not have sufficient endurance to intercede until a delayed answer comes.

THE HIGHEST PRAISE

One of the most notable changes in the life of the student who has recently received the baptism in the Holy Spirit is his worship. He experiences a new freedom and joy in expressing praise. The devotional exercise of tongues can be a beautiful means of worship as the Spirit carries the tongue past the human limitations of thought and expression. Such pure worship is the highest praise.

From the lips of the Spirit-filled student—alone or in the company of others, either speaking "in the Spirit" or with the mind, either in silence or in loud expression, either with singing or plaintive prayer—should regularly flow the highest worship and praise. Engaging in such worship and praise is no selfish pastime, but the result of an infilling with the very Spirit of God.

There is a time for prayer and for intercession. But there must also be times for participation with the angels of heaven in worship, which will be our occupation throughout eternity. The highest praise or worship, then, is that abandoned release, that complete yielding of oneself to the Holy Spirit and allowing Him to lift praise and glory to the Father and the Son. Jesus Christ is the center of our worship. But the Holy Spirit helps the Spirit-filled believer give Jesus the highest praise.

DIVINE GUIDANCE AND DIRECTION

"When he, the Spirit of truth, comes, he will guide you into all truth" (John 16:13). This guidance comes mainly through the illumination of God's Word. But the Holy Spirit also faithfully guides us in matters that are not specifically covered in Scripture. As the mind of Christ dwells within us, we can prayerfully and confidently make decisions and take steps of faith through the Spirit's quiet prompting. If our hearts are sensitive to the Spirit's gentle checks and genuinely thankful for closed doors, we can live with the assurance that the Spirit's guidance is always there when we need it.

A young lad was greatly puzzled by the testimony of adult Christians who said God had spoken to them and told them to do or say a particular thing. Trying to be a good Christian, he listened as intently as he knew how, but he never heard God's voice. He read many accounts of spiritual giants who stepped out in faith at the "word of the Lord" and accomplished great things for God. And he recognized that the Bible was full of instances where God spoke to people. But still he could not hear even a whispered Voice.

✳ As he grew older and matured in the Christian walk, he came to understand a truth that escapes many people, sometimes for an entire lifetime. He learned that, for him, God's voice came in a growing inner conviction rather than a vocal sound or dramatic emotion. He learned to recognize and obey that voice and observed God's hand working supernaturally in his life.

God does speak when we listen, and we have the glorious privilege of divine guidance in every area of our lives. Yes, some people live on impulse, but impulses must be carefully checked to make sure they are really the voice of God and not the human spirit. The devil moves people on sudden impulse to do something odd, but God always gives us time for consideration and the growth of an inner conviction. The Spirit of God works dramatically through the Christian made sensitive by a Spirit-filled life.

The Holy Spirit uses several means to bring this inner conviction into the believer's heart. Your students can know the will of God for their lives through the Scriptures, through prayer (and sometimes fasting), and through circumstances and wise counsel from mature believers. God can use one or more of these means when the believer's heart is yielded to and filled with the Spirit.

Spiritual Maturity—Edifying the Body

The teacher should be the student's model of what the Holy Spirit can make of a person as well as what the Spirit can do through that person to edify and strengthen the body of Christ. But spiritual maturity is not a goal for just the teacher and other leaders in the church. Every Christian is required to become more like Christ. Students must be urged and challenged to grow to spiritual maturity. Not to grow is to slip back into immature actions and responses.

The Holy Spirit seeks to develop each believer to build and

edify the entire Church. *Every* member of a congregation or Sunday school class should edify each other. If the teacher has taught his students properly, he should regularly hear of ministry occurring between class members outside the classroom. In one couples class, members are encouraged to get together during the week for fellowship and sharing. Out of these associations grow relationships that are specially used of the Spirit when one member goes through a hard trial or crisis. In a growing Sunday school class, the teacher cannot be the sole channel of edification. The Spirit, whose ministry knows no time or location restrictions, wants to touch lives through a variety of yielded instruments.

The teacher must instruct the class concerning the gifts of the Spirit and how they are exercised both inside and outside the church. But unless Spirit-filled class members are in interactive and interrelational contact with others, they do not have opportunity to let the Holy Spirit work through them in edifying others.

A real mark of spiritual maturity is the move from self-centered concern ("What can the Holy Spirit do in my life and for my needs?") to concern for ministry to others ("What can the Holy Spirit do through me to meet the needs of others around me?"). We need to spend more time learning and practicing the concepts of 1 Corinthians 12 and 14, tempered by the love emphasis of chapter 13. The gifts of the Spirit are given for the edification of the body of Christ. Every Spirit-filled believer is a member of Christ's body and should make definite contributions, prompted by the Holy Spirit, to the spiritual growth of others.

Leading the Student Into the Baptism Experience

The New Testament does not contain a single instance (after the Day of Pentecost) of a person seeking for long periods of time to be baptized in the Spirit. So the question can properly be asked, "Why do so many believers pray so long before receiving the infilling?"

It is possible there were such instances in the Early Church that were not recorded. Furthermore, we might expect that the great faith and spiritual power of the apostles created great expectancy among believers. The initial outpouring of the Spirit in the Early Church may have been given special impetus by its proximity to the ministry, death, resurrection, and ascension of Jesus. Nevertheless, these possibilities should not detract from the fact that many people today wait longer than necessary before receiving the Baptism. The cause for the delay, in some cases, could be inadequate instruction as well as a lack of expectancy on the part of the recipient.

How can the teacher help the student receive the infilling at the earliest opportunity?

First, the Baptism should be more than just another nice-to-have spiritual experience. It was commanded by Jesus: "Receive the Holy Spirit" (John 20:22) and by Paul: "Be filled with the Spirit" (Ephesians 5:18). The temptations and demands our students face today make the infilling of the Spirit an absolute necessity.

Second, be sure the student has repented and asked forgiveness for his sins. That does not mean that he is perfect; the Spirit comes to help us in our weakness. But we cannot be filled with the Spirit if we knowingly retain sinful habits and mental reservations.

Third, dispel fear. Fear is contrary to faith. Some believers may be afraid of the supernatural working of the Holy Spirit because they do not understand His person and ministry. Jesus knew that men would have this reaction in the face of divine Omnipotence, so He gave an illustration of the Father's love: "If a son asks for bread from any father among you, will he give him a stone? Or if he asks for a fish, will he give him a serpent instead of a fish? . . . [H]ow much more will your heavenly Father give the Holy Spirit to those who ask him!" (Luke 11:11,13, NKJV).

Fourth, help your students receive the baptism in the Spirit by faithfully teaching all the truth about the Holy Spirit. Some instruction does not register the first time it is taught. But as the Spirit anoints the Word, as the promise is faithfully and patiently taught and retaught, the desire for the Spirit's fullness will develop.

Fifth, create expectancy and faith. Relate to your students your own story of questioning, searching, struggling, and finally receiving. Or if you received the Baptism the first time you asked, enthusiastically tell them about the experience. Stories from the Bible, coupled with current testimonies, create expectancy and faith.

Sixth, lead your students in praise and worship. Probably the greatest help we can provide is to surround the seeking believer with an atmosphere of worship and faith. The praise, however, must be genuine, not just the saying of words to encourage the seeker. In instances where a believer has repeatedly asked for the fullness of the Spirit but has not yet received, the act of sincere praise and worship will often lead to speaking in another language. The Holy Spirit especially desires to help us praise and glorify the Father and the Son.

Finally, avoid misleading the seeker. In their desire to see another believer filled with the Spirit, well-intentioned helpers may actually hinder the seeker. Constant instructions as to what to do or say (e.g., repeating certain words or sounds) will more often hinder than help. The formal act of laying on hands may or may not be appropriate, depending on the circumstance and the seeker. But it is always appropriate to demonstrate support and love by your presence and prayer. Remember, it is Jesus who baptizes in the Holy Spirit, not the helper praying with the seeker.

Wherever I Go, the Spirit Goes Too

A humorist once shared a great truth when he said, "Wherever I go, *I* go too, and spoil everything." Our own efforts are not only weak and inadequate, but often seem to spoil everything. We get ourselves into big trouble without even trying.

But for Spirit-filled Christians—your students—the truth is much more positive: "Wherever I go, the Spirit goes too, and blesses everything." Remember that the next time you walk into your classroom, Teacher.

NOTES

[1]Jonathan Edwards, *Religious Affections,* ed. John E. Smith (New Haven, Conn.: Yale University Press, 1959), p. 163.

8

The Holy Spirit and the Teacher

LEROY R. BARTEL

Marg did what few other middle-aged housewives could—she effectively taught a class of junior high boys. Her formal education was limited, but she loved God, His Word, and that class of boys. Her effectiveness came by the help of the Holy Spirit, diligent study, and a consistent Christian life.

At first Len emphatically refused when the pastor approached him about teaching a Sunday school class. He was a dairy farmer not a teacher! But after praying about it, Len finally agreed to help his wife in the primary class. Teaching was not as difficult as he thought it would be. He loved the kids, and they responded to him. One week Len even worked up the courage to volunteer to tell the Bible story. The kids loved it, and so did he. A year later Len was lead teacher of the primary department and convinced he had found his place of ministry in the body of Christ.

I am challenged by what the Holy Spirit can do through lay teachers and workers in the church. Len and Marg are just two examples of many whom God has used to bring life, vitality, and growth to the church. God sent the Holy Spirit to help ordinary people be effective in His work!

LeRoy Bartel, M. Div. with a concentration in Christian education, is coordinator of Christian education and assistant professor at Southwestern Assemblies of God College, Waxahachie, Texas.

What relationship ought to exist between the Holy Spirit and the teacher? How dominant should the role of this member of the Trinity be in teaching?

False Views of the Holy Spirit's Role

Roy B. Zuck highlights four false views of the Holy Spirit and His relationship to the teacher.[1]

The first false view is that the Holy Spirit makes the human teacher unnecessary. The Holy Spirit is the only teacher needed. Any human element is looked upon with suspicion as a contaminating and polluting influence. This view is definitely antiintellectual and is often held by ultrasupernaturalists.

The second false view asserts that the Holy Spirit is a substitute for human effort. This view is similar to the first but does not deny the need for the human teacher. This approach questions the value of study and preparation and discounts educationally sound practices. Teaching, according to those who hold this view, should come directly through the Holy Spirit. The human instrument is used, but is passive.

A third error insists the Holy Spirit simply adds a spiritual footnote to the teacher's work. In this view the Spirit does His part only after the teacher has done all he can. This approach to teaching is really no different from the non-Christian's except that the teacher prays for God to bless, or anoint, his efforts.

The fourth error regards the Holy Spirit as totally unnecessary to the teacher in his task. Those who hold this view take a position diametrically opposed to the first two views. They completely exclude the need for the supernatural element in teaching. Teachers with this view are convinced that with the proper training, proven learning theory, clear and measurable objectives, well-constructed lesson plans, and creative methods and materials, Christian education can be accomplished. The task, as they see it, is educational not spiritual.

A Proper View of the Holy Spirit's Role

How then should we view the relationship between the Christian teacher and the Holy Spirit? What should characterize the divine-human process we call Christian education? Perhaps the following diagram will help.

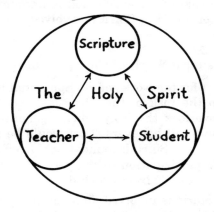

In the vital, dynamic Christian education setting, the teacher and student are involved in a dialogue with each other around the Word of God. However, the Word is not a passive component. "The word of God is living and active" (Hebrews 4:12). The teacher and student communicate with each other and with God, who through His Word speaks to them and confronts them. The Holy Spirit provides the personal, dynamic, all-encompassing context that brings life, vitality, and the possibility of dramatic, miraculous life-change in keeping with God's will.

Teachers need to be prepared, Spirit-filled, and dependent on and sensitive to the work of the Spirit in the teaching-learning process. True, the students have needs and spiritual hunger, but they can also make contributions that result in exciting growth and mutual discoveries. Therefore, the student should not be viewed as the *object* of instruction, but a *participant* in shared learning and discovery.

The Scriptures speak to us because they are inspired by the

Holy Spirit and the message is illuminated through the work of the Spirit. It is essential, therefore, that all Sunday school curriculum be centered in the Scriptures, exegetically oriented, and life-related. The Holy Spirit should be sought and invited into the entire teaching-learning process. He should provide the dynamic context in which God is encountered and lives changed. When the Holy Spirit is involved the possibilities are unlimited!

The General Work of the Spirit in the Teacher

In our quest for the works of the Spirit that are particularly applicable to the task of the Christian teacher, we may be tempted to overlook the Holy Spirit's general work common and available to all believers. That would be a mistake. The general work of the Spirit is foundational to effective teaching. The teacher's participation in the general work of the Spirit becomes the reservoir from which dynamic ministry flows.

The Holy Spirit is involved, first, in bringing spiritual life into being (1 Corinthians 6:11; 2 Thessalonians 2:13,14; Titus 3:5; 1 Peter 1:2). Teachers must know the life-transforming power of being "born from above" and "born of the Spirit" (John 3:5–8). Zuck observes,

> Only teachers who are regenerated by the Spirit of God . . . begin to qualify to do Christian teaching. To neglect this distinctive is to destroy the lines of demarcation between mere religious education and true Christian education. . . . God's plan is to teach through regenerated personalities whom He indwells.[2]

Fred Dickason says, "Regeneration creates a new capacity to think, feel, and perform with God. It renews the moral base of personality and allows both learning and teaching to be carried on through the Spirit."[3]

Second, the Spirit gives the special sense of belonging to God—the inner witness of sonship (Romans 8:15,16; Galatians 4:4–7) and the sealing of the Spirit (2 Corinthians 1:21,22; Ephesians 1:13,14). The Spirit dwelling within makes these things real (John 14:15–18; 2 Timothy 1:14; 1 John 3:24; 4:13). Christian teachers need to have a deep-seated confidence about who they are in Christ. This assurance creates a healthy spiritual self-image that provides a strong base for effective ministry.

The baptism in the Spirit is available to all believers and supplies indispensable power for productive ministry (Matthew 3:11; Mark 1:8; Luke 3:16; Acts 1:4,5,8; 2:1–4). Jesus referred to the filling of the Spirit as though it provided the appropriate uniform for the Christian worker. He spoke of being "clothed with power from on high" (Luke 24:49). The individual believer is to be a temple filled with His presence (1 Corinthians 6:19). Jesus said the Spirit would be "streams of living water" flowing from within (John 7:37–39) and the Father's "good gift" to those who ask for it (Luke 11:13).

In light of this, is it any wonder that Paul urged, "Be filled with the Spirit" (Ephesians 5:18)? A. Skevington Wood comments:

> The theological implications of "be filled" *(plērousthe)* are crucial for a biblical doctrine of the Holy Spirit. The imperative makes it clear that this is a command for all Christians. The present tense rules out any once-for-all reception of the Spirit but points to a continuous replenishment (literally, "go on being filled").... Finally, the verb is passive: "Let yourselves be filled with the Spirit." This is not a manufactured experience.... There may ... be successive fillings of the Spirit; indeed, the Christian life should be an uninterrupted filling.[4]

The Spirit-filled life is an experience and manner of living so vital that no Christian teacher can afford to be without it! The Book of Acts is a historical commentary on what can be accomplished with the Spirit's power.

The Holy Spirit provides resources for living the Christian life victoriously (Romans 8:14–17; Galatians 4:4–7; 5:16–25). The Christian teacher must teach this by example. Consider some of the resources: inner strength (Ephesians 3:16); a new context of freedom out of which to respond to God and His revelation that leads to a transformed life (2 Corinthians 3:14–18); a new attitude toward life characterized by enthusiasm, peace, joy, and hope (Romans 7:6; 8:11; 12:11; 14:17; 15:13; Galatians 5:5; 6:8,9; 1 Thessalonians 1:6); the leading of the Spirit (Romans 8:14); assistance in prayer (Romans 8:26,27); and the "sword of the Spirit"—God's Word—to help us in ministry and spiritual warfare (Ephesians 6:17; 2 Timothy 3:16; Hebrews 4:12; 2 Peter 1:21). Second Peter 1:3 sums it up this way, "His divine power has given us everything we need for life and godliness."

Another of the general activities of the Spirit is His presence and work within the local church. This is very significant to Christian teachers because teachers are gifts God has given to the Church and their calling operates within the context of the church (Ephesians 4:11–16). All Christians are a part of the Church, the collective temple where God's Spirit dwells and manifests itself (1 Corinthians 3:16; Ephesians 2:13–22). The fellowship we enjoy is in the Spirit (Philippians 2:1,2). Any manifestations of the Spirit are for the benefit of the church as a whole (1 Corinthians 12:7).

Character and the Spirit

Character is critical to dynamic teaching. Teachers who make a life-changing impact on their students have discovered it takes more than words to do it. Modeling, a key concept that is receiving attention in educational circles, involves demonstrating the life-change or behavior the teacher desires in the students.

The Holy Spirit works within our lives to produce Christlike character. Galatians 5:22,23 gives a beautiful summary of these character qualities, referred to as the fruit of the Spirit. Each of the qualities cited by Paul in this passage has special significance for the Christian teacher.

1. *Love,* the supreme character quality, is inclusive of all the rest (see 1 Corinthians 13). The church desperately needs teachers who love unconditionally and self-sacrificially.

2. Students need to see genuine *joy* modeled by their teachers. This spiritual quality must not be polluted by the feverish quest for pleasure and selfish happiness we observe in the world around us. Real joy can be found only in the Lord (Philippians 3:1). It finds its most powerful expression in serving the Lord regardless of the circumstances of life (Psalm 100:2; Romans 14:17; 15:13; 1 Thessalonians 1:6; Philippians 1:25).

3. *Peace* does not depend on conducive circumstances for its existence. The Spirit-filled teacher radiates a settled sense of confidence and well-being and responds in a calm, quiet way regardless of the pressure or provoking comment or question. (See John 14:27; Philippians 4:6,7.)

4. *Patience* ("long-suffering," KJV) reveals itself under provocation. What an essential attribute for a teacher with an unruly child or disruptive teen!

5. *Magnanimity* is a word that could be used for the character quality of *kindness*. To be magnanimous is to respond graciously to meanness or misrepresentation.

6. *Goodness* is nobility of character. It projects no taint of a better-than-thou attitude but simply desires to be like Jesus.

7. The *faithfulness* ("faith," KJV) spoken of in Galatians 5 is practical in its expression. It is faith that is lived by—put into action—every day. The teacher who expresses it will not fail God, his class, or his church. It is the opposite of the character quality that always has the teacher reading the whole lesson from the quarterly or calling for a substitute.

8. *Gentleness* ("meekness," KJV; "humility," TEV) is not weakness! This quality of character produced by the Spirit is marked by a "sane estimate of [its] capabilities" (Romans 12:3, Phillips). It is not threatened by the knowledgeable student. The teacher who possesses this quality is comfortable encouraging others as well as making his own contribution.

9. *Self-control* ("temperance," KJV) involves cooperating with God to control one's emotions, desires, thoughts, and behavior. In our "instant-gratification" society, teachers exhibiting this

quality are desperately needed in our Sunday school class-rooms.

The Holy Spirit as Helper

The Greek word *Paraclete* has rich significance for the teacher. Four passages in John's Gospel are especially important to our discussion of this term for the Holy Spirit (John 14:16–18; 14:26; 15:26; and 16:7–16). In the King James Version the word is translated "Comforter." In the newer versions the two words most often used are *Helper* and *Counselor.*

Paraclete is a compound word in the Greek and conveys the idea of calling or summoning someone to the side of another for the purpose of aiding him.[5] Stanley Horton explains the term's significance in *What the Bible Says About the Holy Spirit:*

> The Holy Spirit in John . . . is the Teacher, the Repre-sentative of Christ seeking to convince men of the truth and bring them to repentance. . . . He is the One who teaches them what to say so they will glorify Christ and give Him witness, instead of defending themselves (Luke 12:12). In fact, He is in no way an Advocate or legal Counselor to the disciples, but the Teacher who speaks for Christ and completes His revelation. . . .
> [W]e see in the Comforter the combination of the ideas of a Teacher and Helper who mediates the truth of Christ and gives power for the spread of the gospel and the growth of the Church.[6]

The Holy Spirit is a helper and teacher for Christian teachers today. The significance of what God has revealed in His Word, insight into its implications and application, and the joy of personally discovering its truth are all brought about by the Holy Spirit. Good teachers, in turn, should pray, plan, and structure opportunities for the Holy Spirit to do the same mi-raculous work in the minds and hearts of their students.

The Holy Spirit and the Anointing

If you were to ask a group of Pentecostal Christians what is important for an effective teaching ministry in the church, somewhere high on the list would be "the anointing." Frequently used in Pentecostal churches, this term has rich significance but is often misunderstood. Priests and kings in the Old Testament were set apart by anointing for their special tasks (Exodus 28:41; 29:7–9; 1 Samuel 9:15,16; 10:1; 16:1–3, 11–13).

Jesus applied the term to himself in the synagogue in Nazareth, quoting Isaiah 61:1,2. The anointing was a metaphor used to describe the presence of the Spirit that resulted in a special setting apart and equipping with power for ministry (cf. Acts 10:38). Thus Jesus of Nazareth became known as the *Messiah* (the Hebrew term) or the *Christ* (the Greek term)—God's anointed one.

This imagery has significance for believers today. God anoints believers—setting them apart and equipping them by the Holy Spirit for special tasks. In this sense it is correct to think of teachers as needing the anointing.

The anointing is not a feeling that comes and goes but an *abiding* reality in the teacher's life. Our awareness of God's presence working with us in ministry may fluctuate, but that does not negate the constancy of His presence and power. First John 2:26,27 says,

> I am writing these things to you about those who are trying to lead you astray. As for you, the anointing you received from him remains in you . . . . His anointing teaches you about all things[;] that anointing is real, not counterfeit (cf. John 14:16,17).

The abiding anointing of the Holy Spirit enables us to discern whether or not something is in keeping with God's revealed standards.

The Holy Spirit and the Teacher's Calling

Teachers need to have a sense of calling to their task and ministry. The Scriptures teach both a general calling and a specific calling. The general calling, issued through the Holy Spirit, provides a backdrop against which to understand and appreciate a specific calling. The general calling accents God's continuing purposes for us regardless of the particular area of service to which we are specifically called.

Because of the Spirit's general calling we understand who we are in Christ and the Lord's ultimate claim on our lives (1 Corinthians 1:26–31).

We are called to

salvation and eternal life (Luke 5:31,32; 1 Thessalonians 2:12; 2 Thessalonians 2:13,14; 1 Peter 2:9)

adoption as His sons and daughters (Romans 1:6,7; 9:22–26)

discipleship (Mark 8:34–38)

participation in the rich blessings of His kingdom (Matthew 22:1–14)

the fellowship of His Son (1 Corinthians 1:9)

His purpose (Romans 8:28–30)

holiness (1 Thessalonians 4:7)

peace (Colossians 3:15)

freedom (Galatians 5:13)

participation in Christ's glory and excellence (2 Peter 1:3)

Christlike behavior during persecution, suffering, and trials (1 Peter 2:21–25)

Ultimately we are called to heaven (Ephesians 1:18; 4:4; Philippians 3:14; Hebrews 3:1; 1 Peter 5:10). What a marvelous calling! Little wonder that Paul urges us to "live . . . worthy of our calling" (Ephesians 4:1–3; 1 Thessalonians 2:12).

If the Bible reveals a general calling, it also teaches a specific calling. Paul believed he was specifically called to be an apostle (Romans 1:1; 1 Corinthians 1:1). He even believed that God, in His foreknowledge, had established His will for Paul before the apostle's birth (Galatians 1:15,16). Persons in a teaching ministry in the church need to feel that they have been specifically called to teach. They must have a sense of mission, a sense of accountability to God (1 Corinthians 9:16,17).

The Holy Spirit is intimately involved in extending God's call. When Paul and Barnabas responded to the specific call of God at Antioch, the Holy Spirit said, " 'Set apart for me Barnabas and Saul for the work to which I have called them' " (Acts 13:2). The Spirit's involvement in the call is further confirmed when the writer says they were "sent on their way by the Holy Spirit" (v. 4).

How can an individual know if he has been called to teach? First, potential teachers need to be aware that God calls in a variety of ways. Sometimes the call is extraordinary and miraculous. Other times it may simply be a growing, unavoidable sense that teaching is what the person should do. Both are the authentic call of God.

Second, God will speak to and through others to confirm one's call to teaching ministry. These are wonderful experiences, but it should be noted that confirmations are not calls—only God can call a person.

Third, God's call usually starts where the person is, doing what he can for the Lord (1 Corinthians 7:17–24). God leads from there, sovereignly, providentially, progressively, and supernaturally.

Finally, a person will have gifts that lend themselves to the teaching ministry. The principle is clear and absolute: Those whom God calls to a particular ministry, He gifts to do it effectively. C. Peter Wagner observes,

> It is helpful to recognize that a person's "call" and his or her spiritual gifts are very closely associated.... God does not give gifts which He does not "call" the recipient to use, nor does He call someone to do something for Him without equipping that person with the necessary gift or gifts to do it.[7]

The Gift of Teaching

What is a spiritual gift? Wagner defines it as "a special attribute given by the Holy Spirit to every member of the body of Christ according to God's grace for use within the context of the Body."[8]

Teaching is such a gift! It is mentioned in all the key passages dealing with spiritual gifts in the New Testament (Romans 12:3–8; 1 Corinthians 12:1–31; Ephesians 4:11–16). The importance of teaching to Jesus, the apostles, and the Early Church, cannot be overemphasized. Teaching is mentioned directly or alluded to as often as preaching. In fact, the words *teach* and *preach* are used coordinately (Matthew 4:23; 9:35; 11:1; Acts 15:35; 2 Timothy 1:11, NKJV). The same information used in preaching can be used in teaching (cf. Matthew 28:19,20; Mark 16:15).

Just as prophecy and exhortation are gifts of the Spirit, teaching is a gift and must, therefore, edify or build up the Church. Christian teachers have a responsibility to the Lord and to the church to prepare themselves to do a quality job of instruction.

The church leadership must carefully avoid any hint of an anybody-can-teach attitude. Biblically, if teaching is a spiritual gift, then not just anybody can teach. Many churches are filled with frustrated workers trying to fulfill ministries to which they have not been called and for which they are not gifted. Emergencies may arise that require someone to perform a task to which he is not called or gifted, but that should be the exception, not the rule. The church should consistently help believers discover their place in the body of Christ and conscientiously seek to equip them to fill it.

How does a Christian who desires to serve evaluate whether or not teaching is his spiritual gift? Several factors should be used to assess this.

1. The person considering teaching should pray about it, asking the Lord to lead him and confirm His will.

2. He should be willing to try teaching. He might start as an aide or helper and try different teaching tasks.

3. He should have a desire to teach and find deep personal satisfaction in doing it.

4. He should have a natural love for study, preparation, and planning.

5. He should love working with people and seeing them grow, develop, and find their place in the body of Christ.

6. He should have evident abilities to teach, resulting in people learning and responding to truth.

7. His calling should be confirmed by the church.

The church should not lightly choose its teachers. They should be individuals the church has prayerfully observed, carefully selected, and adequately trained. The action of church leadership in appointing them ought to communicate, "We believe you are called and gifted to teach!"

Some have assigned so great a role to the Holy Spirit in communicating truth that the human teacher of God's Word is ignored. Others have so emphasized educational methodology that the role of the Holy Spirit has been overlooked. Neither of these approaches is adequate to produce the results God desires. The appropriate balance includes a teacher and student interacting with God's Word in a context in which the Holy Spirit is dynamically active.

The Holy Spirit is absolutely essential to the life and ministry of the effective Christian teacher. He does a general work in the life of the teacher—common to all believers—that provides an important foundation for all effective teaching ministry. The Holy Spirit works to develop the teacher's character so that he can effectively model the Christian way of life and deal with students in a Christlike way.

As the *Paraclete* (Helper), the Holy Spirit makes Jesus real and convinces men of truth. The Spirit's anointing sets apart and equips the teacher for ministry. Through the Holy Spirit the teacher is called and gifted for his task. God uses ordinary people, called and empowered by the Holy Spirit, to do mighty things for Him through the ministry of teaching.

NOTES

[1]Roy B. Zuck, *Spiritual Power in Your Teaching,* rev. ed. (Chicago: Moody Press, 1972), pp. 59–65.

[2]Ibid., pp. 17,18.

[3]C. Fred Dickason, "The Holy Spirit in Teaching," *Introduction to Biblical Christian Education,* ed. Werner C. Gaendorf (Chicago: Moody Press, 1981), p. 117.

[4]A. Skevington Wood, "Ephesians," *The Expositor's Bible Commentary,* ed. Frank E. Gaebelein (Grand Rapids: Zondervan, 1978), p. 72.

[5]Marvin R. Vincent, *Word Studies in the New Testament,* vol. 2 (Grand Rapids: Eerdmans, 1946; reprint 1973), pp. 243,244.

[6]Stanley M. Horton, *What the Bible Says About the Holy Spirit* (Springfield, Mo.: Gospel Publishing House, 1976), pp. 122,123.

[7]C. Peter Wagner, *Your Spiritual Gifts Can Help Your Church Grow* (Ventura, Ca.: Regal Books, 1979), pp. 41,42.

[8]Ibid., p. 42.

9

The Holy Spirit and the Task of Teaching

LEROY R. BARTEL

What an exciting and challenging ministry to teach the Bible in the local church! The teacher's text is the greatest Book ever written. Classes are made up of the greatest people in the world—God's people from all age-groups and backgrounds. Leading God's people to maturity is the greatest task a person could have. The assignment to "make disciples of all nations, . . . teaching them to obey everything I have commanded you" (Matthew 28:19,20) can be accomplished only by the greatest power available, the Holy Spirit.

Just exactly what is the Spirit's function in teaching? What resources does He provide for the teacher's preparation and presentation?

What Is Teaching?

What comes to your mind when you hear the terms *teaching* and *teacher* as they relate to the church? Do you see a person standing behind a lectern speaking to a group of people who are sitting in a semicircle listening to him? Or perhaps the picture that comes to your mind is of a group of small children sitting on the carpet around a teacher as she tells them a Bible story.

Is anything wrong with these mental pictures? Absolutely not! Are they totally accurate pictures of what is involved in teaching? I think not.

Several well-known authors on the subject of the church's teaching ministry and the use of spiritual gifts within the church have described teaching in the following ways:

Roy Zuck says, "The gift of teaching is a supernatural, Spirit-endowed ability to expound (explain and apply) the truth of God. . . . [T]eaching is the gift of systematic instruction and application in the doctrines (or teachings) of God's truths."[1]

Charles and Win Arn and Donald McGavran make this statement about teaching as a gift: "Those with the gift of teaching are responsible for preparing and presenting the lesson every Sunday. . . . Teachers' time is spent primarily in study and lesson preparation."[2]

C. Peter Wagner defines the gift of teaching as "the special ability that God gives to certain members of the Body of Christ to communicate information relevant to the health and ministry of the Body and its members in such a way that others will learn."[3]

What do these descriptions of the spiritual gift of teaching have in common? How do they relate to the mental images of teaching that many people have? In each case the primary emphasis is on teaching as a *presentation*.

Although these definitions are good, I believe the biblical model of Spirit-led and empowered teaching is broader. More attention needs to be paid to discovery, participation, and relationships in teaching. I would like to offer the following description based on Wagner's definition of Christian teaching: The gift of teaching is a special ability God gives certain members of the body of Christ to creatively structure and competently guide learning experiences for students of all ages and interests so they are led to discover the meaning of the Scriptures, apply the truth to their lives, and respond appropriately to the message.

The Holy Spirit and Preparation

Effective teachers are prepared teachers, and preparation is work! Preparation involves the best the teacher has to offer in study, planning, and creativity. The Spirit-filled teacher, however, will not think of preparation as merely a human activity. The Holy Spirit should be invited into the task. His presence and abilities should be requested at every step of the process. The Christian teacher should move ahead in the preparation process confident of the Holy Spirit's presence and help.

The Holy Spirit is indispensable in the study of the Scriptures. It would seem only reasonable that the same Spirit who prompted men to pen inspired words should be involved in the process of seeking to understand and apply those words. The Holy Spirit's presence is not a substitute for diligent study, but an enabler of it. Paul urged Timothy, "Be diligent . . . handling accurately the word of truth" (2 Timothy 2:15, NASB). The same advice applies to Spirit-filled teachers today.

When approaching any Scripture passage a key word is *observation*. The Spirit of God is able to sensitize the teacher's eyes to observe what God has inspired. The question that should be answered is "What does the passage say?" Key words should be noted and defined, remembering that a word's meaning is determined by its use in context, not primarily by word-study books. Observation is essential to detecting a passage's key idea and understanding how the writer developed his thought. Study the surrounding text to determine what it contributes to the message. The objective is not to get something out of the passage, but simply to discover what it says.

Interpretation is the teacher's next task. The objective is to discover what the passage meant to those who originally heard it, or what God was trying to communicate to those who experienced what the Bible describes. No attempt is made to look for a new truth or a hidden idea, but simply to discover what God originally wanted to communicate.

Since God's Word was communicated to real people in real situations, discovering the historical, political, spiritual, and cultural situation surrounding the passage is important. Much of this can be gained from an observant reading of the passage itself and its context, but a good commentary can also be helpful. The goal of this stage of study is to enter into the original situation so completely that the full impact of what God said or did is unmistakable and clear. The Holy Spirit will be present to make the truth come alive for the diligent teacher.

After establishing the meaning of a passage, the key task is *application*. The question is, "How does the meaning apply to us?" At this point in study the teacher opens his life to the probing work of the Holy Spirit. The issue is no longer what God was teaching them, back then and there. The focus changes to us, here and now. The Holy Spirit is very application-oriented. He wants to apply the truth in a fresh and vital way to our lives, needs, and situations today.

The final step in the study process is *communication*. As the teacher considers how to pass on the truth God has revealed, he asks himself, "How can I lead the students to discover this for themselves?" Creativity is crucial to this step. But creativity has always been characteristic of the Spirit at work. The teacher who spends time prayerfully reflecting on what he has discovered through studying God's Word will find the Holy Spirit helping him choose creative ways to communicate the message and help the student discover it for himself. The same Holy Spirit who assisted the teacher in the other three steps in the study process—during interaction with God's Word—will help here as well.

The lesson plan should be the fruit of this creative reflection. The Holy Spirit should be involved in its every element. He will assist the teacher in evaluating what to include and exclude in the lesson development. The Spirit will also aid the teacher in choosing creative learning activities to help the students achieve the lesson objectives. A creative climate, produced by the Spirit, should surround and influence every step of the planning.

The teacher should prayerfully formulate learning objectives, or refine and personalize those suggested in the curriculum. Nothing is more frustrating than teaching that goes nowhere. Objectives are simply goals the teacher wants to see accomplished in the students' lives.

God wants to touch and influence three areas of the students' lives with His Word. The first is the *cognitive*—things God wants the students to know or understand. The second is the *affective*—appropriate attitudinal or emotional responses to truth. And the third is the *behavioral*—life-changes that God desires and reveals in His Word.

Knowing, feeling, and doing are all important to God because He is concerned with the entire person. The Holy Spirit will help the teacher develop goals in keeping with the message of His Word in all three areas. The teacher can then especially target one of them based on the needs of his class.

Careful study yields much more material than the teacher can present during a class period, and not all of it is related to the objectives for the day. In addition, a good curriculum includes much more material than the teacher can effectively use. Publishers expect teachers to adapt curriculum to the needs of their class and their lesson objectives.

The same old approach week after week can destroy interest. Any teaching method or learning activity can be overdone. Curriculum writers usually offer the teacher a selection of learning activities to help the students discover the significance of God's Word, reinforce its message, and express themselves in keeping with the truth.

The creative teacher should not be afraid to try something new to help the students discover and apply God's Word. The Holy Spirit is the catalyst of creative ideas. He will help the teacher phrase good discussion questions that probe the heart of important issues. He will suggest exciting approaches to learning that involve the students. Finally, the Holy Spirit will enable the teacher to evaluate and select appropriate activities and then assist in modifying and shaping them to meet the students' needs.

No class is complete without an opportunity to respond to truth. This part of Bible teaching must not be left to chance or haphazardly tacked on at the end of the lesson period. Every passage of God's Word calls for an appropriate response to its message. If a passage is properly taught, the student's response should be, "What am I going to do about it?" An altar call may not be appropriate for every Sunday school class period; salvation is not the only response called for in the Scriptures. Other creative approaches that lend themselves to the interactive class setting can be used. The Holy Spirit will guide the teacher as he prayerfully plans for response.

The Holy Spirit and Presentation

Class presentation is an important part of teaching. Study is basic, providing data for instruction. Preparation involves taking what has been studied and fashioning it into a learning experience, expressed in a lesson plan. Lesson plans are essential, but the task is only partially done when the strategy is on paper. Presentation is the actual initiation of the planned strategy with the students.

The Holy Spirit can enhance the teacher's presentation. Plans should be made, methodology mastered, and public speaking skills improved, keeping in mind, however, that the Holy Spirit is able to lift the teacher's efforts to new levels of effectiveness. He can provide the clarity of thought, the stability of emotions, and the personal poise so necessary to persuasive presentation.

As Pentecostals, we prize a sense of dynamic freedom and sensitive flexibility in our churches. We agree that preparedness is important, but view bondage to notes negatively. Students desire their teacher to be at home enough with the material and the lesson plan, that he can minister to the needs of the class as they emerge. The ability to move away from one's notes—and the lecturn periodically—and look directly at the students is important. The Spirit can set the teacher free from the self-consciousness that prevents him from getting down on the students' level.

Likewise the Holy Spirit is also able to help the teacher maintain a clear objective so that freedom and flexibility do not degenerate into pointless discussions and aimless digressions. The teacher will be able to meet needs creatively without losing a sense of direction.

Class periods have a starting time and a closing bell. It is tragic when, week after week, a teacher barely gets through the lesson's introduction. Realistic time assignments should be jotted in the margin of the lesson plan. Pacing (the judicious management of teaching time) should be practiced. If the teacher asks, the Holy Spirit will nudge him when it is time to move on and will provide wisdom in adjusting minor excesses. If self-control is a fruit of the Spirit—and according to Galatians 5:22,23 it is—then it applies to this concern of teaching.

A sense of appropriate authority comes from the Spirit of God working in the teacher's life. Jesus "taught as one who had authority" (Matthew 7:29; Mark 1:22). At the same time, humility and meekness are virtues of the Spirit. The Spirit-filled teacher should project a blend of these virtues, being humbly assertive and at the same time assertively dependent on the Lord in his ministry.

The teacher must not feel he has to dominate and control every aspect of the class. At the same time, he must not be intimidated. Paul told Timothy, "God did not give us a spirit of timidity, but a spirit of power, of love and of self-discipline" (2 Timothy 1:7). The teacher's poise and confidence do not come from adequate study and preparation alone; the Spirit of God produces these characteristics within the teacher.

Silence does not necessarily characterize a creative learning environment. An effective presentation does not consist of a teacher standing behind a lectern lecturing, while the class listens silently. A dynamic learning environment is characterized by a healthy noise level. When God's Spirit is at work in a classroom there is a buzz of activity—the happy sounds of laughter and creative interaction. Noise does not equal spirituality, but neither does deathly silence.

Classroom management is an important part of a teacher's presentation. An out-of-control class can be as distracting and counterproductive to learning as an unprepared teacher. Many of the problems teachers face can be solved by a well-planned and properly executed lesson plan that moves along without a lot of dead spots or fumbling about.

The teacher's interpersonal skills are critical to dealing with class problems. Firmness, consistency, and loving honesty ought to characterize correction and discipline. Heated differences of opinion that surface in discussion must be defused so they do not become destructive. The Christian teacher must believe the Holy Spirit will help him solve classroom problems by providing the resources necessary to deal with them (cf. Galatians 5:16–25; Ephesians 4:1–3,23–32; Colossians 3:12–14).

The Holy Spirit in the Classroom

In addition to the Holy Spirit's work with the teacher during the preparation and presentation of the lesson, one of the most exciting and dynamic dimensions of His ministry is within the classroom. Apart from the Spirit, the sociological dynamics of a classroom are exciting. Add the personality of the Spirit of God to the learning context and the possibilities are unlimited!

First, the Holy Spirit works with each of the three key participants in the Christian education context to create a vital learning climate in which God can be encountered through His Word. He works within the teacher to enable him to powerfully communicate truth and guide the student's learning experience in such a way that the truth is discovered, applied, and responded to appropriately.

The Spirit works within the student convincing him of sin, righteousness, and judgment (John 16:7–11); revealing Christ to him (John 16:14); and opening his eyes to the significance of revealed truth (1 Corinthians 2:11,12).

But not only is the Holy Spirit at work within the teacher and the student, He also acts upon and through God's Word.

"Living and active" through His ministry (Hebrews 4:12), the Scriptures are more than just curriculum or a textbook, they are the Word of God.

The Holy Spirit not only works with each of these participants and elements, He also works in the dialogue and interaction between them. In a very real sense, the Spirit of God directs the entire learning context. Wielding an unseen but evident influence in the classroom, His goal is life change and growth in the image of Christ.

It would be easy to say the Holy Spirit works to create the ideal learning climate in the classroom. In one sense that is true. But on the other hand, from the teacher's perspective, it is probably best to say there is no ideal learning environment. The Holy Spirit must work with imperfect people with imperfect understanding. If an ideal learning environment is continually sought, the teacher may begin to think that learning can take place only when each of the participants is properly responding to the work of the Spirit and the ideal climate actually exists. Such a state does not occur often, if ever.

At times a dynamic learning climate does exist. The class seems to be especially alert and responsive. As exciting as that situation is, the danger is that we will try to bottle it up, think about what we were doing when it happened, and try to recreate it every week. However, God would remind us that He works with imperfect teachers and students to accomplish His will, and the Holy Spirit is active among us whether or not we feel Him.

What is needed, then, is sensitivity and flexibility on the teacher's part in adjusting to the learners' needs. Creativity and innovation are essential if obstacles in an imperfect learning environment are to be met and overcome. The Holy Spirit is at work making the teacher aware of these factors and enabling him to find imaginative, effective solutions.

The Holy Spirit is at work in both the teacher and the students to produce a number of general characteristics that contribute to a healthy learning environment. The same Holy Spirit who works to make the teacher sensitive to the students' needs is at work in the students to produce a corresponding alertness to, interest in, and hunger for ultimate Truth.

Openness to one another and to the will of God is another work of the Spirit. Mutual acceptance of one another in spite of differences and weaknesses contributes to a context for learning (Romans 14:1; 15:7). Tolerance is a characteristic closely related to this. Of course, the summarizing characteristic of a vital learning environment is love (Colossians 3:12,13). A review of love's characteristics (1 Corinthians 13) and the fruit of the Spirit (Galatians 5:22,23) indicates the Holy Spirit is the key to a dynamic climate for learning.

The classroom can also provide the setting for the miraculous. The Scriptures clearly teach that the manifestations of the Spirit (the word of wisdom, word of knowledge, faith, gifts of healing, working of miracles, prophecy, discerning of Spirits, tongues, and interpretation of tongues) provide supernatural aids to ministry (1 Corinthians 12:8–10). The spiritually informed and alert teacher will recognize God's desire to manifest himself in the class in these ways through both teacher and students. What vitality this will add to a classroom! The overriding principle to guide all spiritual activity is, "To each one the manifestation of the Spirit is given for the common good" (1 Corinthians 12:7).

The Holy Spirit Outside the Classroom

If we are going to practice biblical teaching in the power of the Spirit, Jesus should be our example. Jesus' teaching ministry followed the educational practices of His day. In that time, a person would join himself to a teacher (rabbi or master) and become his disciple. The student spent a great deal of time with his master, sometimes actually living with him. All of life became a classroom. Relationship was a part of the instructional dynamic. Jesus used this approach. He was a discipler.

Jesus' commission to His disciples was, "Go and make disciples" (Matthew 28:19). In saying this, He prescribed a particular model of instruction that was broader than a simple presentation on Sunday. In this mode, relationships outside the classroom are viewed as a part of the total teaching dynamic. More stress is placed on the teacher's modeling Christianity, less on his simply telling a lesson on Sunday. Chance encounters, visitation, and social functions have great significance in a relationship. Interpersonal skills become more important. In short, teaching becomes more than what I do 1 hour a week. It involves what I am.

The fellowship of believers has always been a context in which people have learned the Christian way of life. It is also a context in which God historically has made His presence known (Matthew 18:20; 1 Corinthians 5:4). For teachers who are involved in the disciple-making business, His promise is, "Surely I will be with you always, to the very end of the age" (Matthew 28:20; cf. John 14:16–18)—a clear reference to the Holy Spirit's presence and power. The Holy Spirit is at work in relationships as we go about making disciples. He desires to use the teacher outside the classroom!

Teaching is more than presentation, it involves creating learning experiences in which students can discover scriptural truth and apply and respond to it in a context in which God's Spirit is active. The Spirit's involvement in the teaching task is pervasive! He is vitally engaged with the teacher in preparation (including the study and planning stages) and presentation. Within the classroom, He is at work using the ministry of the teacher and the Word to create a vital learning climate for the student. Outside the classroom, the Spirit of God is at work in relationships as teachers seek to obey their Lord and make disciples.

NOTES

[1]Roy B. Zuck, *Spiritual Power in Your Teaching,* rev. ed. (Chicago: Moody Press, 1972), p. 70.

[2]Charles Arn, Win Arn, and Donald McGavran, *Growth: A New Vision for the Sunday School* (Pasadena, Ca.: Church Growth Press, 1980), p. 132.

[3]C. Peter Wagner, *Your Spiritual Gifts Can Help Your Church Grow* (Ventura, Ca.: Regal Books, 1979), p. 127.

10

The Teacher—Perpetuator of the Pentecostal Heritage

G. RAYMOND CARLSON

You have had an overview of the Pentecostal revival, including the person and work of the Holy Spirit through the curriculum, teacher, and student in the Sunday school. Now we come to responsibility—yours and mine—for today and tomorrow. We must move from retrospect to prospect.

Our founding fathers adopted a simple Statement of Faith that has withstood the tests of time and the attacks of doctrinal aberration. The Assemblies of God movement has weathered every onslaught of the archenemy of the Church since the Fellowship was organized in 1914. This is largely due to the fact that we have remained true to the Bible as "our all-sufficient rule for faith and practice." The Movement has remained committed to the Pentecostal distinctive (Acts 2:4), which sets us apart from non-Pentecostal groups.

Commitment is a key word if we are to perpetuate our faith and heritage. Commitment implies obligation, responsibility, assurance, and resolution.

Committed to the Lordship of Christ

To perpetuate our faith and heritage we must be committed to the lordship of Christ. A Spirit-led teacher gladly acknowledges Jesus as Lord.

G. Raymond Carlson is general superintendent of the Assemblies of God, Springfield, Missouri.

The most important truth in relation to Christian experience is the lordship of Christ. Jesus' great objective in all His redemptive work was that He might be Lord in the life of every redeemed person (Philippians 2:6–11). In loving recognition of His work in redemption—whether men agree or not—God has made His Son "both Lord and Christ" (Acts 2:36; cf. Romans 14:9).

The acceptance of Christ as Savior involves a recognition of Him as Lord, for the One who saved us has the right to be the Sovereign in our life. In a very real sense the primary purpose of our Lord's death and resurrection was not so much saviorhood as sovereignty. True, He came to save us from our sins, but the ultimate purpose was that He might be our Lord.

He has been constituted Lord by divine decree. His right to lordship over our lives is not based on recognition of it, but on God's recognition of His mediatorial work. His lordship is not only declared but deserved. He not only deserves this position, but also earnestly desires it. To refuse Him is to rob Him of the fruit of His passion.

What does His lordship mean to us? It begins with the recognition of His absolute ownership (Acts 10:36). He is Lord of all that I am and all that I have. Everything that I am and that I possess is His by right of creation and purchase.

His lordship profoundly affects my whole Christian life. I have been "chosen in the Lord" (Romans 16:13). I have been called "by the Lord" (1 Corinthians 7:22). I became a Christian on the terms of Romans 10:9: "If you confess with your mouth, 'Jesus is Lord,' and believe in your heart that God raised him from the dead, you will be saved." As a Christian, I am sanctified by setting "apart Christ as Lord" in my heart (1 Peter 3:15).

All of my service for Christ is "labor in the Lord" (Romans 16:12, KJV). I live and move and have my being in the Lord. "Whether we live, we live unto the Lord; and whether we die, we die unto the Lord: whether we live therefore, or die, we are the Lord's" (Romans 14:8, KJV). Even in passing from this life our death is "in the Lord" (Revelation 14:13).

Christ's lordship is not only something I must recognize, but also something I must feel. If He is Lord, He of necessity takes up every part of me—head and heart, intellect and feeling, body, soul, and spirit.

Christ's lordship also implies complete submission. My will, my ambitions, my desires are set aside as I submit to Him. All resistance, all rebellion to His will must be laid at His feet.

Christ's lordship implies unquestioning obedience. " 'Why do you call me "Lord, Lord," and do not do the things which I say?' " (Luke 6:46, NKJV). No matter how strange or difficult His commands may seem, we do well to heed the words of Mary at the wedding at Cana: "Whatever He says to you, do it" (John 2:5, NKJV). Disobedience invalidates all alleged acknowledgment of His lordship.

Christ's lordship implies wholehearted service. When Isaiah "saw" the Lord, he realized his own unworthiness, but as he "heard" the Lord, he responded to the "voice of the Lord . . . . 'Here am I. Send me!' " (Isaiah 6:1–8). Join with Paul in total surrender saying, " 'Lord, what do You want me to do?' " (Acts 9:6, NKJV).

Christ's lordship also implies complete trust. Can we say with Job of old, "Though He slay me, yet will I trust Him" (Job 13:15, NKJV)? Service out of self-will brings failure, but recognizing the Lord turns failure to victory. The barren results of self-will experienced by the disciples in John 21 were turned around as they found their answer, "It is the Lord" (v. 7).

Committed to the Authority of the Word

To perpetuate our faith and heritage, we must be committed to the authority of God's Word. The Bible is the authoritative, inspired, infallible, and inerrant revelation of God.

The spiritual problem of our day is *authority.* The dictionary defines authority as "the right to command and to enforce obedience; or the power to determine, on the ground of knowledge, credibility, or character." The authority of the Bible is that quality by which it demands faith and obedience to all its declarations.

There are three basic positions with regard to the authority of the Scriptures. The rationalist exalts human reason to the throne of final arbitration and rebels against the thought of an authoritative book. But to exalt man's reason is to overlook the fact that since man is a sinner his very thought processes are influenced by sin, which is in the very heart of his being. (Note Paul's answer in 1 Corinthians 2:14.)

A second position is that the church is the final authority. Proponents of this view argue that the church gave us the Scriptures and has been the custodian of Holy Writ. But we respond by stating that the church did not give us the Bible, and even though the writers of the New Testament were members of the Church, God used them as individuals. The Word did not come into being through a church or a church council. God is the originator (2 Peter 1:21).

The Assemblies of God and evangelicals take the third position, assigning to the Bible absolute supremacy as the only rule of faith and conduct and the only test of truth. The unique authority of the Bible must be linked to the unique authority of Christ.

The Bible speaks with no less authority than that of the Divine Voice. Its words (i.e., language) are the words of men; its word (i.e., message) is the Word of God. For men to claim that the Bible is nothing more than a book of inspired words is to miss the miracle of its origin and the marvel of its unity. It is the Word of God in human language. Infallibility, inerrancy, or veracity do not account for the inspiration of the Bible. They are understood only in terms of inspiration: Because the Scriptures are inspired by the Holy Spirit they are infallible and inerrant.

Committed to Doctrinal Purity

To perpetuate our faith and heritage we must be committed to doctrinal purity. What a person believes is important. What a church teaches is important. The New Testament, and especially the pastoral letters of Paul, give frequent reference to doctrine. "Give attendance . . . to doctrine . . . . Take heed . . . unto the doctrine" (1 Timothy 4:13,16, KJV). "The time will come when they will not endure sound doctrine" (2 Timothy 4:3, KJV). "Teach what is in accord with sound doctrine" (Titus 2:1).

Doctrine is necessary to communicate the Christian faith. We must be able to communicate truth. Doctrine is also necessary to defend the Christian faith. The Christian needs to know how "to answer everyone" (Colossians 4:6) and "be prepared to give an answer to everyone who asks . . . the reason for the hope that [he has]" (1 Peter 3:15). Believers "should earnestly contend for the faith which was once delivered unto the saints" (Jude 3, KJV).

Doctrine is important and we must maintain doctrinal purity. "Sound doctrine" is in contrast to unhealthy teaching. The apostles not only taught truth but also contended for its purity against any who would corrupt it.

Error and truth travel side by side in the marketplace, in the dwelling place, and even in the holy place. Error is so skilled at having the appearance of truth that the two are often mistaken. Often error is embraced because it is so well represented. False teachers beguile unstable people with "great swelling words" (2 Peter 2:18; Jude 16, KJV).

Truth and error are too serious to permit leniency. The New Testament makes no room for erroneous thinking and false teaching. Truth produces results and error always takes its revenge.

Overemphasis of a Bible truth, at the expense of taking it from its context or failing to balance it with the entire teaching of the Scriptures on the subject, leads to error. Error that persists becomes a cancer.

Certainly living the Christian life is more important than knowing Christian doctrine, but there would be no Christian experience if there were no Christian doctrine. We need clear-cut beliefs to have clear-cut convictions.

Committed to the Person and Work of the Spirit

To perpetuate our faith and heritage we must be committed to the person and work of the Holy Spirit.

The Holy Spirit is the Executive of the Godhead. Through the Spirit God created and preserves the universe. Through the Spirit God became incarnate in human flesh. Through the Spirit God works, converting sinners and sanctifying and sustaining believers.

The Spirit proceeds from God, is sent by God, and is God's gift to us. How He can be one with God and yet distinct from the Father and the Son is one of the mysteries of the Trinity. Human wisdom can never understand the Almighty. The unity—and the separateness—of the Father, Son, and Holy Spirit stand as an eternal paradox, defying finite comprehension. Ignorance and neglect of the person and work of the Holy Spirit are so prevalent that many church members would have to say with the people at Ephesus, "We have not even heard that there is a Holy Spirit" (Acts 19:2).

The full manifestation of the Spirit's personality and deity, the full meaning of His equal position in the Godhead, and the clear-cut scope and objective in His work are declared in the New Testament. Truth concerning the Spirit forms a major theme in almost every New Testament book.

Many times during the centuries God had manifested His presence on earth, but the divine visitation of the Holy Spirit recorded in Acts 2 was different from all His other appearances. The Holy Spirit had come to stay with believers. Jesus had promised that the Comforter would come to "abide with [us] for ever" (John 14:16, KJV).

If the Holy Spirit is not allowed to actively direct the operation of the church by controlling the lives of its members, the church will have lost its dynamic. We may have a great deal of activity, but Christian character is not produced by human prowess. Even though we may be doctrinally correct, what value does that have if we do not know and have the presence of the Holy Spirit in power?

It is imperative that we maintain our Pentecostal distinctive. If we do not hold to our position regarding speaking in other tongues as the initial physical evidence of the baptism in the Holy Spirit, we have in essence lost our reason for being a Pentecostal church.

Committed to the Great Commission

To perpetuate our faith and heritage we must be committed to the Great Commission. Both soul winning and discipling are involved.

SOUL WINNING

Christianity is a personal matter. Christ comes to dwell in us individually. As an individual, you are part of His body. The essence of your Christian experience is "Christ in you" (Colossians 1:27). He indwells us individually to minister through us: "God . . . works in you both to will and to do for His good pleasure" (Philippians 2:13, NKJV).

God seeks to convict people of their sins and convince them of the gospel—that is the work of the Holy Spirit—but He is in you. He works through you. He uses your tongue, your lips, your voice, your body. If you do not witness or tell the message, some will be eternally lost. Christ ordained to live in you, to speak to the lost through you. You are the channel for Him to minister through.

You may memorize the *mechanics* of soul winning, but God wants to give you the *dynamics* of soul winning. There were two types of evangelism in the Apostolic Church: mass evangelism and personal evangelism. The record indicates the importance of the latter. The Apostolic Church was ablaze with personal witnessing. That has always been true of revival movements.

We have no choice. Our Lord's last command was, "Go into all the world and preach the gospel to every creature" (Mark 16:15, NKJV). This is His charge to every one of His followers; one thing we are commanded to do.

God has placed you where you are to be His contact person to lost men and women. Let the Holy Spirit empower you to be an effective witness for Christ. He is Christ's gift to you to give you the needed power and guidance. Depend on the Spirit to open the door to another's heart. Expect Him to prepare the soil (heart) of the unsaved person to receive the seed of God's Word by your witness. Few joys can be greater than bringing people to Christ.

Keep your vision fresh. Sense the heartbeat of the Savior, which comes by living close to Him. From the intense spirit that Jesus showed in His dealings with people it is quite evident that He expects us to be personal evangelists (Matthew 28:18–20; Mark 16:15–20; Luke 24:46–48). From these passages we clearly understand that Jesus commanded personal evangelism.

The harvest is ripe, but the laborers are few. You and I must not miss the golden opportunity of gathering sheaves for our Lord and Master before it is eternally too late.

DISCIPLING

Discipleship is a part of the Great Commission. Evangelism is twofold. First, we must make new converts. Then we must instruct, develop, and disciple them. The latter is less exciting than the first. Too often we stop in midcourse. We enlist disciples but leave the development to others. One of the weakest links in many churches is the lack of fervency in nurturing converts.

"Make disciples" is one of our Lord's most important commands to us. The word *disciple* in its various forms occurs about 275 times in the four Gospels and the Book of Acts. The word means a learner, as contrasted to a teacher. But, as used by our Lord, it implies more than being a student; it also entails being a follower. A student focuses on the material learned; a disciple focuses on following a person, the teacher. Loyalty is an important part of being a disciple.

Jesus used a simple, direct call: "Follow Me" (Matthew 9:9; Mark 2:14). Study the calls He gave to various individuals. He offered a new life through loyalty to Him. They did not know what the call entailed, but trusted that He would make it worthwhile.

Our Lord defined discipleship in several ways.

1. Cross bearing is implied. "Whoever does not bear his cross and come after Me cannot be My disciple" (Luke 14:27, NKJV).

2. A disciple submits all to God. Stewardship replaces ownership. "Whoever of you does not forsake all that he has cannot be My disciple" (Luke 14:33, NKJV).

3. A disciple lives in God's Word. Jesus said, "If ye continue in my word, then are ye my disciples indeed" (John 8:31, KJV).

4. A disciple loves his fellow Christians. "By this all will know that you are My disciples, if you have love for one another" (John 13:35, NKJV).

5. A disciple lives a fruitful life. "Herein is my Father glorified, that ye bear much fruit; so shall ye be my disciples" (John 15:8, KJV).

These characteristics identify a person as a disciple of Christ. Note them again: self-denial and cross bearing, abiding, sacrificial love, fruit bearing, and the surrender of material possessions and existing relationships. They yield rich rewards in this world and in the world to come (Mark 10:29,30).

The second half of the Great Commission charges us to teach those we win to Christ to obey everything He commanded (Matthew 28:20). In the King James Version, the word "teaching" in verse 20 means to give instruction, whereas the word "teach" in verse 19 means to enroll or enlist disciples ("make disciples," NIV, NKJV). We are to instruct and "build . . . up" (Acts 20:32) new converts. That is what Paul means in Colossians 2:6,7: "Just as you received Christ Jesus as Lord, continue to live in him, rooted and built up in him, strengthened in the faith as you were taught."

Committed to the Church

To perpetuate our faith and fellowship we must be committed to the Church. The Church is a divine institution planned by God the Father, founded by God the Son, and empowered by God the Holy Spirit. The Church is divine at the point of her origin. She is divine in the content of her continuing purpose. She is divine in her ultimate goal.

God places a very high value on the Church. Value is determined by several criteria, such as purchase price, function, and utility. That is how we value our personal possessions. That which costs us little or nothing is rarely held in high esteem. That which offers little utilization is likewise of little value to us.

The Church has such high value to God and to believers because it was purchased at an infinite price, the price of Jesus' precious blood. Let me ask, Shall I—shall you—count a thing small for which the Son of God paid the awful price of His own shed blood?

When people lose sight of the purchase price of the Church, they lose respect for it. The apostle Paul's profound respect for the Church was based on recognition of the fact that it is the purchased possession of Christ.

The Church's greatest function and utility is that it serves as a glorious habitation of God through the Spirit.

The Church is the vehicle God has chosen to use to spread the gospel.

The Church is a shining light in the darkness of a crooked and perverse generation, standing as a bulwark against the onslaughts of immoral filth which seeks to engulf our world.

The Church serves as a custodian to preserve the gospel in its pristine simplicity, all the while earnestly contending for "the faith which was once delivered unto the saints" (Jude 3, KJV).

The Church serves as a protection for believers. As an ark it provides safety; as a sheepfold it provides shelter; as a Good Samaritan it binds up the wounds of those robbed and left for dead.

The Church furnishes a community of fellowship for believers with God and with one another.

The Church is the only institution in the world that deals with the souls of men. The Scriptures clearly indicate the place of the local church in God's scheme of things. As Billy Graham has said, "Only evangelism done through the Church can be conserved by the church." The importance of the local church cannot be overemphasized.

Committed to Holy Living

To perpetuate our faith and fellowship we must be committed to holy living. Holiness is the ideal that God has in mind for every believer. God himself is "glorious in holiness" (Exodus 15:11, KJV) and He has called the redeemed to this "because it is written, Be ye holy; for I am holy" (1 Peter 1:16, KJV).

To be holy means very simply that Christ's character becomes visible in our lives. We belong to God and as such we are the body of Christ. The transforming grace of God comes to change us. We are to be transformed into the image of Christ, and His character is the best description of holiness to be found.

Some hide behind the grace of God to excuse their lack of holy living. But "cheap grace" is not grace; it is a perversion of grace. To those who receive Him, Christ gives the "power to become the sons of God" (John 1:12, KJV). To those who obey Him, Christ gives the power to become the saints of God. We are called to be saints and, as such, Christ delights to share His power through the Spirit to make us what we were intended to be.

God commands us to be holy, but that holiness is not self-produced, it is Spirit wrought. As a new person in Christ Jesus, the believer is to walk in newness of life, putting "on the new man, which after God is created in righteousness and true holiness" (Ephesians 4:24, KJV).

Committed to Fellow Believers

To perpetuate our faith and fellowship we must be committed to one another. One of the marks of the followers of Jesus was their love for each other. People know that we are His disciples if we "love one another" (John 13:34,35).

The phrase *acid test* is used concerning the genuineness of something. In Jesus' statement quoted above, He gave the acid test of Christianity, the criterion by which people know the genuineness of the Christian's testimony. Love for the Lord and for fellow believers is the grand distinctive that defines, denotes, and distinguishes Christians from all other religions, creeds, and schools of thought.

We are known by what we show, or demonstrate. Love will always reveal itself; it cannot be hidden. Love is the true gauge to measure spiritual growth.

The Bible commands, "Consider how we may spur one another on toward love and good deeds" (Hebrews 10:24). We are also told, "Each esteem others better than himself" (Philippians 2:3, NKJV).

Jesus outlined disciplines for His disciples in the Sermon on the Mount (Matthew 5:1–12). He calls us to be willing to give up our rights (v. 5), to be willing to get involved in other people's hurts (v. 7), to learn the art of making peace (v. 9), and to handle offenses constructively (vv. 10–12).

Revival movements have always encouraged a caring spirit in the lives of those who have responded to the Holy Spirit. May we never allow materialism and creature comforts to make inroads into our lives so that we lose our dependence on and love for one another. Paul expected to find Timothy "with the brethren" (1 Corinthians 16:11, KJV).

Committed to a Teaching Ministry

To perpetuate our faith and fellowship you, as a teacher, must be committed to your calling.

Satan wrestles for the souls of our youth in unmasked fury (2 Timothy 3:2–4). Meanwhile, some churches think that religious education is nothing more than child care. Tragically, many students never gain a personal appreciation for their parents' faith. As a result, they opt for the world. Parents and teachers cannot isolate their children and students from the world, but they can enable them to cope with its allurements.

As a teacher you have an awesome responsibility and a golden opportunity. Allow the creative genius of the Holy Spirit to work in and through you. Model by example what the Bible teaches regarding a follower of Christ. Study *what* to teach, not only *how* to teach. Teach the Word of God. Use innovative methods, but don't sacrifice content. Surely the teacher whose heart is aflame with the spiritual content of the lesson should rise above the professional attitude of those who deal in mundane matters.

By teaching our Movement's past, you as a teacher can ensure that new generations will not only catch the vision, but also enlarge it. For to be a teacher is to be a runner between history and the future—not simply bearing the flame of our heritage, but passing its baton as well.